The AI-Enabled Executive

Written By
Bradley J. Martineau

Disclosure And Legal Disclaimer

This book is intended solely for educational purposes and does not constitute legal, business, financial, or investment advice. The content within this book is based on the author's research and personal experiences and should not be relied upon for making legal, business, financial, or investment decisions or taking legal, business, financial, or investment actions on your behalf or on behalf of an organization. Readers are strongly encouraged to always consult with a competent attorney to obtain specific legal advice tailored to their individual circumstances and to always seek professional advice from qualified financial and investment advisors.

Furthermore, any business, financial, or investment advice provided in this book is for informational purposes only and does not guarantee any specific results. The author and publisher disclaim any liability for any losses or damages incurred as a result of applying the information contained in this book. Readers should perform their own due diligence and seek professional advice before making any business, financial, or investment decisions.

Investing in financial markets involves significant risks, including the potential loss of principal. The information provided here is for

About The Author

As an AI executive consultant, Mr. Martineau leverages his vast business and legal experience to help executives in navigate complex business landscapes, offering strategic advice on AI integration as to corporate governance, risk management, privacy policies, and operational efficiency. He prides himself on helping executives to overcome complex AI challenges as well as seize unique opportunities that it opens up. His hands-on approach and dedication helps them to drive their organizations towards sustained growth and success.

He also shares trending, insightful, and actionable AI strategies for executives through dynamic speaking engagements that are tailored to help leaders thrive in today's fast-paced, AI technologically driven, and ever-evolving business world. He educates leaders on the AI business platforms that are already having a significant beneficial impact for organizations as well effective prompt engineering on generative AI models, such as Perplexity, ChatGPT, and CoPilot.

Prologue

In the archives of human history, few technological advancements have captivated the imagination and sparked as much excitement and apprehension) as artificial intelligence (AI). Once the stuff of science fiction, AI has swiftly transitioned from the fringes of possibility to the forefront of reality, permeating nearly every facet of our lives. The transformative power of AI promises to reshape the very fabric of business, society, and our daily existence as we know it.

This book is not merely a guide to understanding AI as an executive; it's an invitation to embark on a journey—a journey that will take you through the intricacies of AI technology, its applications, and its profound impact on an organizational landscape. It's a journey that challenges us to rethink traditional business models, innovate with purpose, and embrace a future where AI is an indispensable and critical ally.

The promise of AI lies in its ability to augment human capabilities, turn data into actionable insights, and automate mundane tasks while freeing us to focus on creativity, strategy, and innovation. Some people think that AI actually does more than just augment human capabilities, such as Darryl Anka when he channels Bashar. He says on AI, and I am paraphrasing, that when we engage with AI, we are essentially engaging with a higher form of ourselves. No matter what your viewpoint on what AI actually is, we do know for a fact that it is a very powerful and transformative tool that is only getting better, and with great power comes great responsibility.

In these pages, you will discover how executives are harnessing AI to drive operational efficiency, enhance customer experiences, and pioneer new frontiers. You will learn about the skills required to thrive in an AI-driven economy, the importance of continuous learning, and strategies for preparing your workforce for the AI transition. Through case studies, practical insights, and expert perspectives, *The AI-Enabled Executive* aims to demystify AI for you and provide a roadmap for leveraging its full potential. Be sure to reference and learn the "Glossary of Key AI Terms" at the end of the book, especially if AI is fairly new to you.

You will notice that throughout the book, endnotes, where I cite the articles and books at the end of the sentence, paragraph or section as the source of the concepts and statements presented therein. These articles and books at the end of the book are great additional sources for you as they provide a much more in-depth analysis on the specific topics being discussed by some of the best educators, leaders, and technological minds.

Finally, I used AI as a virtual assistant in writing this book. Specifically, I used it to help (1) brainstorm and outline topics, (2) edit, (3) research the books and articles that I used as my research, (4) research the AI platform examples provided throughout and (5) help write the "Glossary of Keywords."

As we navigate the complexities of this technological revolution, one thing is certain, AI is not a fleeting trend but a fundamental shift that will shape the future of work, commerce, and personal endeavors. The road ahead may be filled with challenges, but it's also brimming with opportunities for those willing to learn, adapt, innovate, and lead!

Table of Contents

Chapter 1:
The Historical Context Of AI Development

In the dawn of the artificial intelligence (AI) revolution, organizations around the world find themselves on the brink of unprecedented transformation, where intelligent machines are set to redefine the very essence of innovation and efficiency. This paradigm shift is not merely a technological evolution but a fundamental change in how enterprises operate, compete, and grow. As AI permeates every sector, from healthcare to finance and retail to manufacturing, it brings with it the promise of unparalleled advancements in data analysis, decision-making, and automation. Executives are now ready to harness the power of AI to gain deeper insights into consumer behavior, streamline operations, and develop products and services that were once beyond the realm of possibility.

However, this new frontier also demands a reevaluation of workforce dynamics, ethical considerations, and strategic planning. In this transformative era, executives must navigate the complexities of AI integration, balancing the benefits of automation with the imperative of maintaining a human touch in their customer interactions. The AI revolution is not just about adopting new technologies; it's about envisioning a future where intelligent systems and human ingenuity converge to create a more efficient, innovative, and prosperous world.

The historical context of AI development is a fascinating journey that spans centuries, beginning with ancient myths and early mechanical inventions and evolving through groundbreaking research in the mid-20th century to the sophisticated AI systems we see today. Early civilizations imagined intelligent beings, such as the Greek myth of Talos, a giant automaton made of bronze, reflecting humanity's long-standing fascination with creating life-like machines.[i]

This curiosity continued into the Renaissance, with inventors like Leonardo da Vinci designing mechanical devices that mimicked human and animal actions. The mid-20th century marked a significant turning point with the advent of modern AI, driven by pioneers like Alan Turing, who laid the theoretical groundwork for machine intelligence. The subsequent decades saw the rise and fall of AI research, punctuated by periods of intense innovation and "AI winters" of reduced funding and interest.[ii]

Early Concepts and Pioneers

The early concepts and pioneers of AI laid the foundational theories and innovations that have shaped the development of AI, setting the stage for the technological advancements we are witnessing today.

The roots of artificial intelligence can indeed be traced back to ancient history, with myths and stories from various cultures depicting mechanical beings and artificial constructs designed to emulate human behavior and thought, like the bronze giant Talos, which was said to guard the island of Crete, and similarly, in Chinese mythology, the figure of Yan Shi was known for creating an artificial humanoid.[iii]

However, the field of AI as we know it began to take shape in the mid-20th century, propelled by the convergence of theoretical concepts and technological advancements. One of the seminal figures in this evolution was Alan Turing, a British mathematician and logician whose work laid the foundation for modern computer science and artificial intelligence.[iv]

Turing's landmark paper, "Computing Machinery and Intelligence," published in 1950 in the journal *Mind*, posed the provocative question: "Can machines think?" In this paper, Turing introduced the concept of the "imitation game," now famously known as the Turing Test. The test involves a human judge engaging in a conversation with both a human and a machine designed to generate human-like responses. If the judge cannot reliably distinguish the machine from the human, the machine is said to have demonstrated a form of intelligence.[v]

The Turing Test was not just a theoretical exercise; it was a bold challenge to the prevailing notions of intelligence and computation. Turing's ideas highlighted the potential for machines to emulate cognitive processes, and his work fundamentally redefined the boundaries of what machines could achieve. His contributions extended beyond theoretical discourse; as during World War II, Turing played a crucial role in breaking the German Enigma code, demonstrating the practical applications of computational theory.[vi]

The 1950s marked a period of rapid development in the field of AI, driven by a combination of academic research and technological innovation. In 1956, a pivotal event occurred, which was the Dartmouth Conference, organized by John McCarthy, Marvin Minsky, Nathaniel Rochester, and Claude Shannon. This conference is widely regarded as the birthplace of AI as an academic discipline. McCarthy, who coined the term "artificial intelligence," envisioned a new field dedicated to creating machines capable of performing tasks that would require intelligence if done by humans.[vii]

The Dartmouth Conference catalyzed a wave of enthusiasm and research in AI, leading to significant advancements in areas such as problem-solving, natural language processing (NLP), and robotics. Researchers began to explore the possibilities of machines that could learn, reason, and even play games like chess. Early AI programs, such as the Logic Theorist developed by Allen Newell and Herbert A. Simon, showcased the potential of AI to replicate human problem-solving capabilities.[viii]

As the field of AI continued to evolve, it encountered both successes and challenges. The initial optimism of the 1950s and 1960s was tempered by periods of stagnation and setbacks, often referred to as "AI winters." Nevertheless, the foundational work of pioneers like Turing, McCarthy, Minsky, Newell, and Simon provided a robust platform for future breakthroughs to come.

The historical context of AI development is a testament to the enduring quest to understand and replicate human intelligence. From ancient myths to modern-day innovations, the journey of AI is a reflection of humanity's relentless pursuit of knowledge and progress. The pioneering efforts of early thinkers and researchers remain a source of inspiration and guidance as the early concepts and pioneers of AI laid a crucial foundation, driving innovation and establishing the principles that continue to propel the field forward today.

Milestones in AI Research

Significant milestones in AI research highlight key advancements and breakthroughs that have propelled the field of AI forward, shaping its development and impact on various industries. AI research has seen several significant breakthroughs over the decades, each contributing to the advancement of machine learning and deep learning technologies.

Early Neural Networks (1950s-1960s):

The development of early neural networks in the 1950s and 60s provided a primitive model for machine learning. A foundational contribution came from Warren McCulloch and Walter Pitts, who in 1943 published the paper "A logical calculus of the ideas immanent in nervous activity" in *The Bulletin of Mathematical Biophysics*. This work introduced the concept of artificial neurons and laid the theoretical groundwork for neural network research.[ix] One of the earliest implementations was the Perceptron, developed by psychologist Frank Rosenblatt in 1957. The Perceptron was a single-layer neural network designed to recognize binary patterns, and it laid the groundwork for future neural network research.[x] Around the same time, Alexey Ivaknenko developed the Group Method of Data Handling (GMDH), which is considered one of the earliest forms of deep learning. The GMDH algorithm could create models that optimize their complexity to improve prediction accuracy.[xi]

Backpropagation Algorithms (1980s):

In the 1980s, the advent of backpropagation algorithms enabled more effective training of neural networks. This algorithm, which efficiently calculates gradients to adjust network weights and minimize errors, was first introduced by Paul Werbos in his 1974 PhD thesis. However, it wasn't until 1986 that David Rumelhart, Geoffrey Hinton, and Ronald Williams published their seminal paper "Learning Representations by Back-Propagating Errors" in *Nature* that backpropagation gained widespread recognition and adoption in the field of machine learning.[xii]

Emergence of Deep Learning (Early 21st Century):

The early 21st century witnessed the emergence of deep learning, where multilayer neural networks began achieving remarkable success in tasks such as image and speech recognition. A pivotal moment in this era was the development of AlexNet in 2012 by Alex Krizhevsky, Ilya Sutskever, and Geoffrey Hinton. AlexNet significantly outperformed previous models in the ImageNet competition, demonstrating the potential of deep learning for computer vision tasks.[xiii] ImageNet is a large visual database designed for use in visual object recognition software research.[xiv]

These milestones in AI research have paved the way for the development of advanced AI systems that continue to push the boundaries of what is possible in machine learning and AI.

The Evolution of AI Technology

Advancements in hardware and software have played a critical role in the evolution of AI.

Hardware Advancements

The evolution of AI technology has been significantly propelled by remarkable hardware advancements, transforming complex computations from theoretical possibilities into practical applications and driving unprecedented innovation.

The introduction of graphics processing units (GPUs) revolutionized computational power, allowing for the processing of large datasets at unprecedented speeds. Originally designed for rendering graphics in video games, GPUs excel at parallel processing, making them ideal for handling the massive amounts of data required for training deep learning models.[xv] Parallel processing is a method of simultaneously breaking down and processing multiple tasks across various processors to achieve faster computation,[xvi] with there being two primary types, data parallelism and task parallelism.[xvii] NVIDIA's CUDA platform, introduced in 2006, enabled developers to leverage GPUs for general-purpose computing, significantly accelerating AI research and applications.[xviii]

Beyond GPUs, the development of specialized AI hardware such as Tensor Processing Units (TPUs) by Google has further advanced computational capabilities. TPUs are custom-designed to accelerate machine learning workloads, providing significant performance improvements over traditional CPUs and GPUs for specific AI tasks.[xix] Additionally, companies like Intel and AMD have introduced their own AI accelerators, such as the Intel Nervana Neural Network Processor and AMD's Radeon Instinct, to cater to the growing demand for AI hardware.[xx]

Software Innovations

The evolution of AI technology has been profoundly influenced by groundbreaking software innovations, which have enabled more sophisticated algorithms, enhanced learning capabilities, and greater adaptability.

AI Frameworks:

Software innovations have played a crucial role in popularizing AI, making it accessible to a wider range of researchers and developers. Frameworks like TensorFlow, developed by Google, and PyTorch, developed by Facebook's AI Research lab, have become essential tools for building and training machine learning models. These frameworks provide user-friendly interfaces, extensive libraries, and robust support for building complex neural networks, enabling researchers to experiment and innovate with greater ease.[xxi]

Open-Source Ecosystem:

The open-source nature of these frameworks has fostered a collaborative ecosystem where researchers and developers can share their work and build upon each other's contributions. This collaborative environment has accelerated the pace of AI research and development, leading to rapid advancements in the field. Projects such as Keras, an open-source neural network library, have further simplified the process of developing AI models by providing high-level APIs that run on top of TensorFlow and other frameworks.[xxii]

The Interplay Between Hardware and Software

The interplay between hardware improvements and software advancements has continually driven AI forward. Enhanced computational power provided by GPUs and specialized AI hardware has enabled researchers to train deeper and more complex neural networks, leading to breakthroughs in various AI applications. Concurrently, the development of powerful and user-friendly software frameworks has empowered a broader audience to engage in AI research and development, fostering innovation and accelerating progress.[xxiii]

The synergy between hardware and software advancements has been pivotal in the evolution of AI, transforming it from a niche field into a mainstream technology with wide-ranging applications.

AI Winters and Resurgences

The journey of AI has been marked by periods of high expectations followed by disillusionment, known as "AI winters." These periods of reduced funding and interest in AI research occurred when the promises of AI could not be matched by the practical outcomes.

The First AI Winter (1970s):

The first AI winter occurred in the 1970s. During the 1950s and 1960s, there was significant enthusiasm and optimism about the potential of AI, fueled by early successes such as the development of the Perceptron and the General Problem Solver.[xxiv] However, the limitations of early AI systems soon became apparent. The AI programs of that era struggled with complex problems, and their inability to scale up to practical applications led to growing skepticism.[xxv] Additionally, the Lighthill Report, published in 1973, critically assessed the progress in AI research and concluded that AI had failed to achieve its ambitious goals, which influenced the decision of funding agencies to reduce or withdraw financial support for AI research.[xxvi]

The Second AI Winter (Late 1980s to Early 1990s):

The second AI winter occurred in the late 1980s and early 1990s, driven by similar factors. Despite the initial excitement around the development of expert systems in the 1980s, these systems were costly to develop and maintain. They also lacked the flexibility to handle real-world complexity.[xxvii] The collapse of the market for Lisp machines, which were specialized computers optimized for AI research, further contributed to the downturn.[xxviii] Consequently, many companies and research institutions scaled back their AI projects, leading to another period of reduced funding and interest in AI.[xxix]

Resurgences in AI:

However, each winter was followed by a resurgence fueled by new technological breakthroughs and an improved understanding of AI's potential. The resurgence in the late 1990s and early 2000s was driven by advancements in machine learning algorithms, increased computational power, and the availability of large datasets.[xxx] The development of support vector machines and the success of AI in specific applications, such as IBM's Deep Blue defeating world chess champion Garry Kasparov in 1997, rekindled interest in AI.[xxxi]

The most recent resurgence in the 2010s has been characterized by the success of deep learning and big data analytics. The availability of powerful GPUs enabled the training of deep neural networks on large datasets, leading to significant breakthroughs in image and speech recognition.[xxxii] Key developments include the creation of AlexNet, which revolutionized computer vision by winning the ImageNet competition in 2012.[xxxiii] Additionally, the development of frameworks like TensorFlow and PyTorch made AI tools more accessible to researchers and developers, accelerating the pace of innovation.[xxxiv]

This period also saw AI achieving superhuman performance in games such as Go, with DeepMind's AlphaGo defeating world champion Lee Sedol in 2016.[xxxv] The combination of deep learning, reinforcement learning, and big data analytics has demonstrated AI's potential to solve complex problems and deliver practical benefits across various industries.[xxxvi]

Ultimately, the AI winters and subsequent resurgences have played a crucial role in shaping the industry by driving innovation through periods of challenge and renewed momentum.

Chapter 2:
Understanding The Basics Of AI

In this chapter, we lay out the foundational concepts and terminology of AI. By exploring its various forms and methodologies, we aim to demystify the complex world of intelligent systems. We will examine the essential principles that underpin AI, including machine learning, neural networks, and natural language processing (NLP), to provide a comprehensive understanding of how these technologies work.

Additionally, we will look at the crucial role of data in AI, highlighting how data is collected, processed, and utilized to train AI models and enable them to make accurate predictions and decisions. By gaining a solid grasp of these basics, you will be well-equipped to appreciate the transformative potential of AI and its applications in various fields.

Key Concepts and Terminology

Understanding the key concepts and terminology in AI is essential for navigating its complexities, grasping its capabilities, and effectively leveraging its technologies across various domains.

Artificial Intelligence (AI)

Artificial Intelligence (AI) refers to the simulation of human intelligence processes by machines, especially computer systems. These processes include learning (the acquisition of information and rules for using the information), reasoning (using rules to reach approximate or definite conclusions), and self-correction.

Machine Learning (ML)

Machine Learning (ML) is a subset of AI that involves the use of algorithms and statistical models to enable computers to perform specific tasks without using explicit instructions. Instead, systems rely on patterns and inference.

- **Supervised Learning:** The model is trained on a labeled dataset, meaning that each training example is paired with an output label. For example, in a supervised learning task for image classification, a dataset of labeled images (e.g., cats and dogs) is used to train the model to classify new images. Supervised learning is widely used in applications such as email filtering, fraud detection, and medical diagnosis.[xxxvii]
- **Unsupervised Learning:** The model is used on data with no labels and is tasked with identifying hidden patterns or intrinsic structures in input data. For example, clustering algorithms can

group customers with similar purchasing behaviors without prior labels. Unsupervised learning is used in applications such as customer segmentation, anomaly detection, and recommendation systems.[xxxviii]

Deep Learning

Deep Learning is a subset of ML involving neural networks with three or more layers. These neural networks attempt to simulate the behavior of the human brain to learn from large amounts of data. It's particularly effective in tasks like image and speech recognition. For example, convolutional neural networks (CNNs) are used in image recognition tasks, such as identifying objects in photographs. CNNs are a type of deep learning model designed to automatically and adaptively learn spatial hierarchies of features from data. On the other hand, recurrent neural networks (RNNs) are used for sequence prediction tasks like language translation. RNNs are also a type of neural network designed to handle sequential data by utilizing feedback loops, allowing them to maintain a memory of previous inputs and capture temporal dependencies. Deep learning has also been applied to fields such as natural language processing (NLP), autonomous driving, and game playing.[xxxix]

Scalable Linear Models (SLMs)

Scalable Linear Models (SLMs) are a category of traditional ML methods that use linear relationships to model data. They are simpler and less computationally demanding compared to deep learning models. While SLMs are highly efficient for tasks involving structured data and straightforward relationships, deep learning excels in handling unstructured data like images, text, and speech. Linear regression is a foundational SLM used to predict a continuous target variable based on one or more input features. For example, it can forecast housing prices based on factors like square footage, number of bedrooms, and location. It's scalability makes it suitable for large datasets in business analytics or financial forecasting. Logistics regression is another widely used SLM. It predicts binary outcomes (e.g., yes/no, pass/fail) or probabilities. It's often employed in fields like healthcare (e.g., diagnosing diseases based on medical data) or marketing (e.g., determining whether a customer will click an ad). These models are valued for their simplicity, interpretability, and ability to scale to large datasets efficiently.[xl]

Natural Language Processing (NLP)

NLP involves the interaction between computers and humans using natural language. It enables computers to understand, interpret, and generate human language. Applications include language translation, sentiment analysis, and chatbots. For example, Google Translate uses NLP algorithms to translate text from one language to another, while sentiment analysis tools can determine the sentiment behind a piece of text, such as whether a product review is positive or negative. Chatbots like those used in customer service applications leverage NLP to understand and respond to customer queries.[xli]

Computer Vision

Computer Vision is a field of AI that trains computers to interpret and make decisions based on visual data from the world. This includes identifying objects in images, facial recognition, and image generation. For example, self-driving cars use computer vision to recognize traffic signs, pedestrians, and other vehicles on the road. Facial recognition technology is used in security systems to identify individuals based on their facial features and in social media platforms to tag friends in photos.[xlii]

Reinforcement Learning

Reinforcement Learning is an area of ML where an agent learns to make decisions by taking actions in an environment to maximize some notion of cumulative reward. It's used in robotics, gaming, and automated decision-making systems. For example, reinforcement learning algorithms have been used to train AI systems to play and master games like chess and Go, where the AI learns optimal strategies through trial and error. In robotics, reinforcement learning is used to teach robots to perform tasks such as grasping objects and navigating environments.[xliii]

Bias and Fairness in AI

Bias in AI refers to systematic errors that can result in unfair outcomes, such as privileging one group over another. Ensuring fairness involves recognizing and mitigating these biases through diverse training data, transparent algorithms, and regular audits to maintain ethical AI systems. For example, AI systems used in hiring processes must be carefully designed to avoid biases that could disadvantage certain groups based on gender, race, or other factors. Techniques such as bias detection and mitigation, diverse data collection, and algorithmic transparency are crucial for developing fair and ethical AI systems.[xliv]

Different Types of AI

The various types of AI, ranging from narrow to general to superintelligent, each represent distinct stages of technological advancement and capability, playing different roles in automating tasks and solving complex problems.

Narrow AI

Narrow AI systems are designed to perform specific tasks and are already widely used in various applications. Virtual assistant tools like Siri, Alexa, and Google Assistant help users with tasks through voice commands. These assistants can answer questions, set reminders, and control smart home devices, showcasing the practical applications of narrow AI in everyday life.[xlv]

Platforms like Netflix and Amazon use AI to recommend products and content based on user behavior. These systems analyze user preferences and past interactions to suggest movies, books, or products that the user is likely to enjoy. For example, Netflix uses collaborative filtering algorithms to recommend shows based on the viewing history and preferences of similar users.[xlvi]

Facial recognition is used in security systems, social media, and smartphone authentication. For example, Facebook uses facial recognition to suggest tags for friends in photos, and smartphones use it for secure unlocking. Additionally, security agencies use facial recognition technology to identify individuals in surveillance footage.[xlvii]

General AI

General AI, while it's still theoretical, would have the ability to understand, learn, and apply knowledge across a wide range of tasks, which is similar to a human. Its development poses challenges and ethical considerations, such as ensuring it aligns with human values. Achieving general AI would require significant advancements in understanding human cognition and replicating it in machines, such as exhibiting common sense reasoning, contextual understanding, and the ability to generalize knowledge across diverse tasks.[xlviii]

Superintelligent AI

Superintelligent AI represents an intelligence far surpassing human capabilities. It raises significant ethical and existential questions, including control, alignment with human goals, and the potential risks of creating such powerful entities. Discussions around superintelligent AI often involve considerations of safety measures, ethical guidelines, and governance to ensure that such powerful AI systems benefit humanity without posing undue risks. Theoretical discussions suggest that superintelligent AI could solve complex global problems but also highlight the need for robust control mechanisms to prevent unintended consequences.[xlix]

The Role of Data in AI

Data plays a critical role in AI, serving as the foundation for training algorithms, improving accuracy, and enabling intelligent decision-making across various applications.

Data Collection

Data collection is the foundation of AI, involving the gathering of information from various sources, such as sensors, user interactions, and online activities. This data serves as the raw material for training AI models. For example, e-commerce websites collect user data such as browsing history, purchase behavior, and product preferences to personalize shopping experiences. Additionally, IoT (Internet of Things) devices collect environmental data that can be used for smart home automation.[1]

Data Preprocessing

Before data can be used to train AI models, it must be cleaned, transformed, and organized. This includes removing noise, handling missing values, and normalizing data. For example, data preprocessing for a machine learning model might involve removing duplicates, filling in missing values, and scaling numerical features to ensure that the model learns effectively from the data. Data preprocessing is a crucial step to ensure the quality and accuracy of the AI model.[li]

Training Data

High-quality, representative training data is crucial for building effective AI models. The data must accurately reflect the conditions under which the AI will operate to ensure its reliability. For example, training a facial recognition model requires a diverse set of images representing different ages, ethnicities, and lighting conditions to ensure the model performs well across various scenarios. Ensuring the diversity and accuracy of training data helps mitigate biases and improves the generalizability of the AI model.[lii]

Big Data

Big data refers to the vast volumes of structured and unstructured data generated daily. AI systems leverage big data to uncover patterns, make predictions, and inform decisions. For example, social media platforms analyze massive amounts of user-generated content to understand trends, sentiment, and user behavior. In healthcare, big data is used to predict disease outbreaks and personalize treatment plans based on patient data. The ability to process and analyze big data enables AI systems to derive valuable insights and drive innovation across various industries.[liii]

Data Privacy and Security

Ensuring the privacy and security of data used in AI applications is essential. This involves implementing robust data protection measures and complying with all relevant regulations to safeguard sensitive information. For example, organizations must adhere to data protection regulations such as the General Data Protection Regulation (GDPR), which sets guidelines for data collection, processing, and storage. Implementing encryption, access controls, and regular audits helps protect data from unauthorized access and breaches. Maintaining data privacy and security is critical to building trust and ensuring the ethical use of AI.[liv]

Data Annotation

Data annotation involves labeling data to provide context and meaning for AI algorithms. This step is critical for supervised learning, where the AI learns from labeled examples. For example, in a dataset used for training a self-driving car, images might be labeled with information about road signs, pedestrians, and other vehicles. Accurate data annotation is essential for the model to learn correctly and make accurate predictions. The quality of data annotation directly impacts the performance of the AI model.[lv]

Synthetic AI Data

Synthetic AI data is artificially generated data that mimics the statistical properties of real-world data without containing any actual personal or sensitive information. Its created using advanced algorithms, such as generative adversarial networks (GANs) and Variational Autoencoders (VAEs), to simulate realistic datasets. This approach enhances privacy by eliminating the need to use real data, thereby reducing risks of data breaches and ensuring compliance with privacy regulations like the General Data Protection Regulation (GDPR). Synthetic data is particularly valuable in fields like healthcare and finance, where sensitive information must be protected while still enabling robust AI model training and analysis.[lvi]

Feedback Loops

Feedback loops use the outputs of AI systems to continuously improve their performance. By analyzing the results and making adjustments, AI models can evolve and become more accurate over time. For example, a recommendation system might adjust its algorithms based on user feedback, refining its suggestions to better match user preferences. In reinforcement learning, feedback loops enable the AI agent to learn from its actions and improve its strategy to maximize rewards. Continuous feedback and iteration are key to enhancing the effectiveness and adaptability of AI systems.[lvii]

Mastering the basics of AI will help empower you as an executive to harness the amazing potential of the technology to drive innovation and shape a smarter, more efficient future. By familiarizing yourself with the foundational concepts, terminology, and methodologies, you can better appreciate how AI works, and the critical role data plays in shaping intelligent systems. This knowledge provides a solid foundation for exploring more advanced topics and applications of AI in various fields. As we continue to look deeper into the world of AI, we will uncover the immense possibilities it holds and the profound impact it can have on our lives and industries.

Chapter 3:
How AI Is Transforming Industries Today

AI is revolutionizing industries across the globe by automating processes, enhancing decision-making, and driving unprecedented levels of efficiency and innovation. From manufacturing and healthcare to finance and retail, AI technologies are being harnessed to streamline operations, improve accuracy, and unlock new opportunities for growth. By analyzing vast amounts of data, AI enables executives to make more informed decisions, predict trends, and personalize customer experiences.

Let's look closer at these industries and some of the specific AI-driven platforms being used by them.

Healthcare:

AI's impact on healthcare is profound, with applications ranging from diagnostics to personalized medicine. In the realm of diagnostics, AI algorithms are capable of analyzing medical images and data with remarkable accuracy, leading to earlier detection of diseases and conditions, which not only enhances the accuracy of diagnoses but also significantly reduces the time required for medical evaluations. AI-powered tools are being used to develop personalized treatment plans that cater to the unique genetic makeup and medical history of individual patients. By leveraging vast amounts of data, AI can identify patterns and correlations that might be overlooked by human practitioners, thereby resulting in more effective and tailored treatments. Furthermore, AI is revolutionizing patient care by enabling remote monitoring and telemedicine, allowing healthcare providers to track patient health in real-time and intervene promptly when necessary.

AI-Driven Diagnostics

AI-driven diagnostic tools can analyze medical images with high accuracy, identifying conditions such as cancer at earlier stages better than traditional methods. For example, AI algorithms can detect abnormalities in X-rays, MRIs, and CT scans with a high degree of precision. This has led to earlier and more accurate diagnoses, improving patient outcomes and allowing for timely intervention.[lviii] One significant example is the use of AI in mammography, where AI systems have demonstrated the ability to identify breast cancer at earlier stages, thus reducing the need for invasive biopsies.[lix]

A couple of AI-driven diagnostic tools that can analyze medical images are:

- Viz.ai: An AI-powered platform that assists radiologists in analyzing medical images, particularly for detecting abnormalities in chest X-rays and other imaging modalities. It uses advanced algorithms to provide real-time analysis and improve workflow efficiency, aiding in faster and more accurate diagnoses. You can find out more information on Viz.ai, at viz.ai.

- Zebra Medical Vision: Offers AI-driven solutions for medical imaging analysis. It uses machine learning to detect various conditions, such as liver disease, cardiovascular issues, and bone health, from medical images like CT scans and X-rays, aiming to enhance diagnostic accuracy and support clinical decision-making. You can find out more information about Zebra Medical Vision at zebra-medical.com.

Personalized Medicine

Personalized medicine leverages AI to analyze genetic information and predict individual responses to treatments, enabling more tailored and effective therapies. By examining large datasets, AI models can identify patterns and correlations that human analysts might miss, leading to the development of customized treatment plans. This approach, known as precision medicine, takes into account an individual's genetic makeup, lifestyle, and environmental factors to recommend the most effective therapies.[lx]

AI-driven personalized medicine has shown promise in treating various diseases, including cancer, where it helps in selecting the most appropriate chemotherapy drugs for individual patients based on their genetic profiles.[lxi]

A couple of AI-driven platforms that analyze large datasets to identify patterns and correlations to provide customized treatment plans are:

- IBM WatsonX for Healthcare: Uses AI and machine learning to analyze vast amounts of healthcare data, including medical records, clinical trials, and genomic data. It helps healthcare providers identify patterns and correlations to develop personalized treatment plans for patients, and it provides insights into disease progression, treatment efficacy, and patient outcomes. You can find out more information on IBM Watson for healthcare at ibm.com.

- Tempus: An AI-enabled platform that focuses on precision medicine by analyzing clinical and molecular data. It uses machine learning algorithms to identify patterns and correlations in patient data, helping healthcare providers develop customized treatment plans. You can find out more information on Tempus at tempus.com.

Administrative Efficiencies

Administrative efficiencies are also enhanced through AI-powered systems that streamline scheduling, billing, and patient record management. These systems can automate routine administrative tasks, freeing up professionals to focus on more critical and complex aspects of their work, such as strategic planning, decision-making, and engaging with patients. For example, AI can optimize appointment scheduling by predicting no-shows and suggesting optimal times for appointments, thereby reducing wait times and increasing efficiency.[lxii] Additionally, AI-powered electronic health records (EHR) systems can help in organizing and retrieving patient information more efficiently, improving the accuracy of medical records and facilitating better care coordination.[lxiii]

A couple of AI-driven platforms that can streamline medical scheduling, billing, and patient record management are:

- Hyro: An AI-powered platform that automates scheduling, maximizing provider capacity and optimizing appointment volumes. It offers features like self-rescheduling, appointment verification, and cancellation management. It integrates with electronic medical records (EMR) systems to provide seamless scheduling across multiple channels, improving patient satisfaction and reducing administrative burdens. You can find out more information on Hyro at hyro.ai.

- Athenahealth: A cloud-based platform that leverages AI to streamline medical billing and coding processes. Its advanced algorithms analyze claims data to identify errors, reduce denials, and ensure compliance with regulations. It also offers real-time insights into revenue cycles and integrates with patent record management systems to enhance overall efficiency. You can find out more information on Athenahealth at athenahealth.com.

AI's transformative impact on healthcare is reshaping the industry in remarkable ways. By enhancing diagnostic accuracy, enabling the development of personalized treatment plans, and facilitating remote patient monitoring, AI is revolutionizing patient care and medical practices. The integration of AI into healthcare is driving significant improvements in patient outcomes and operational efficiency while also opening new avenues for innovative solutions. As AI technologies continue to advance, their role in healthcare will only grow, further solidifying their importance in delivering high-quality, patient-centric care that meets the evolving needs of our society.

Finance:

In the financial sector, AI is driving a paradigm shift by revolutionizing a wide array of functions, from fraud detection to algorithmic trading and customer service. In fraud detection, AI systems analyze vast amounts of transaction data in real-time to identify unusual patterns and flag potentially fraudulent activities, thereby enhancing the security and integrity of financial transactions. Algorithmic trading, powered by AI, enables the execution of complex trading strategies at lightning speed, leveraging predictive analytics to make data-driven decisions that maximize returns and minimize risks.

AI is also transforming customer service by employing chatbots and virtual assistants to provide personalized support, swiftly addressing customer inquiries and offering tailored financial advice. By automating routine tasks and augmenting human capabilities, AI not only improves operational efficiency but also creates a more secure and responsive financial ecosystem.

Fraud Detection

AI and machine learning algorithms have transformed the way financial institutions detect and prevent fraud. By analyzing vast amounts of transaction data, these algorithms can identify unusual patterns and anomalies that may indicate fraudulent activity. For example, machine learning models can detect subtle changes in spending behavior, geographic inconsistencies, and other red flags that human analysts might overlook. This not only enhances the security of financial transactions but also helps in reducing the financial losses associated with fraud. Financial institutions like banks and credit card companies leverage AI to continuously monitor and analyze transaction data in real-time, ensuring prompt detection and response to fraudulent activities.[lxiv]

A couple of AI-powered fraud detection platforms for financial institutions are:

- Darktrace: An AI-driven cybersecurity platform that uses machine learning to detect and respond to cyber threats, including fraud. It analyzes network traffic and user behavior to identify anomalies and potentially fraudulent activities in real-time. Its technology helps financial institutions protect against various types of fraud, such as account takeovers and insider threats. You can find out more information on Darktrace at darktrace.com.

- Kount: An AI-enabled fraud prevention platform that specializes in detecting and preventing online fraud. It uses machine learning algorithms to analyze transaction data, device information, and user behavior to identify and block fraudulent activities. Its platform is widely used by financial institutions to protect against payment fraud, account takeover, and other types of online fraud. You can find out more information on Kount at kount.com.

Algorithmic Trading

Algorithmic trading systems use AI to make real-time trading decisions based on market data, optimizing investment strategies. These systems can process and analyze large volumes of financial data at high speeds, allowing them to execute trades faster and more accurately than human traders. By incorporating machine learning algorithms, algorithmic trading systems can identify market trends, predict price movements, and optimize trade execution strategies. This not only improves the efficiency of trading operations but also enhances profitability. High-frequency trading (HFT) is a prominent example of algorithmic trading where AI algorithms execute thousands of trades per second based on real-time market data.[lxv]

A couple of AI-driven algorithmic trading systems that are:

- TrendSpider: An AI-powered trading platform that uses machine learning algorithms to analyze market data and identify trading opportunities. It offers features like automated technical analysis, backtesting, and real-time alerts. TrendSpider's AI Strategy Lab allows users to create and test trading strategies without needing to code, making it accessible for traders of all skill levels. You can find out more information on TrendSpider at trendspider.com.

- Trade Ideas: An AI-driven platform that uses advanced algorithms to scan the market and suggest real-time trading opportunities. It provides features like AI-generated trade ideas, backtesting, and risk management tools. Trade Ideas' AI, named Holly, analyzes millions of trading scenarios every night to identify the best opportunities for the next trading day. You can find out more information on Trade Ideas at trade-ideas.com.

INVESTING DISCLAIMER: Investing in financial markets involves significant risks, including the potential loss of principal. The information provided here is for informational purposes only and should not be construed as financial, investment, or legal advice. Be sure to perform your own due diligence before making any investment decisions. Past performance is not indicative of future results. Always seek the counsel of a qualified financial advisor or other professional to determine the appropriateness of any investment strategy or transaction for your personal circumstances, but ultimately, any investments you make are made at your own risk.

Customer Service

AI-powered chatbots and virtual assistants are revolutionizing customer service in the financial sector. These AI systems provide instant support to customers, handling a wide range of inquiries from account balances and transaction histories to loan applications and investment advice. By automating routine customer service tasks, AI chatbots reduce the workload on human agents, thereby allowing them to focus on more complex and value-added services. This not only enhances the customer experience by providing timely and accurate responses but also reduces operational costs for financial institutions. Additionally, AI virtual assistants can offer personalized financial advice by analyzing customer data and providing tailored recommendations.[lxvi]

A couple of AI-driven chatbots are:

- IBM WatsonX Assistant: A powerful AI customer service chatbot platform that uses natural language processing (NLP) to understand and respond to queries. It can be integrated into various channels, including websites, mobile apps, and messaging platforms. Watson Assistant is known for its ability to handle complex conversations, provide accurate responses, answer FAQs, and provide personalized responses. You can find out more information on IBM WatsonX Assistant at ibm.com.

- Google Cloud Dialogflow: An AI chatbot platform that enables organizations to build conversational interfaces for websites, mobile apps, and messaging platforms. It uses machine learning to understand user intent and provide relevant responses. It supports multiple languages and can be integrated with various third-party services, making it a versatile option. You can find out more information on Google Cloud Dialogflow at cloud.google.com.

AI's transformative influence in the financial sector is reshaping how financial institutions operate, secure transactions, and interact with customers. By enhancing fraud detection capabilities, optimizing algorithmic trading strategies, and revolutionizing customer service through intelligent virtual assistants, AI is driving unprecedented levels of efficiency, accuracy, and personalization. As AI technology continues to advance, it will further solidify its role as an indispensable tool in the financial industry, paving the way for innovative solutions that meet the ever-evolving needs of the market.

Retail:

AI is reshaping the retail landscape in profound ways, driving significant advancements in how retailers interact with customers, manage inventory, and streamline their supply chains. By leveraging

AI-driven technologies, retailers can provide highly personalized shopping experiences, tailoring product recommendations and promotions to individual preferences and behaviors. This level of personalization enhances customer satisfaction and loyalty, creating a more engaging and enjoyable shopping experience.

Moreover, AI is revolutionizing inventory management by predicting demand patterns, optimizing stock levels, and reducing waste, ensuring that products are available when and where customers need them. In the realm of supply chain management, AI enables greater efficiency and transparency by analyzing vast amounts of data to identify potential disruptions, optimize routes, and improve overall logistics. As AI continues to evolve, its integration into the retail sector promises to drive innovation, efficiency, and customer-centric strategies that redefine the future of retail.

Personalized Customer Experiences

Personalized marketing strategies driven by AI analyze customer behavior to deliver targeted promotions and recommendations, increasing sales and customer loyalty. By leveraging data from customer interactions, purchase history, and browsing behavior, AI can create highly tailored marketing campaigns. These campaigns can include personalized emails, product recommendations, and dynamic pricing strategies that cater to individual customer preferences.[lxvii] For example, retailers like Amazon and Netflix use sophisticated AI algorithms to recommend products and content, enhancing the customer experience and driving engagement.[lxviii]

A couple of AI-enabled platforms that can provide personalized marketing strategies by analyzing customer behavior are:

- Adobe Experience Platform: A comprehensive customer data platform that uses AI and machine learning to analyze customer data from various sources. It helps organizations create unified customer profiles and deliver personalized experiences across multiple channels. The platform's AI capabilities enable real-time data processing, predictive analytics, and personalized marketing strategies based on customer behavior and preferences. You can find out more information on the Adobe Experience Platform at business.adobe.com.

- Salesforce Customer 360: An AI-powered platform that integrates data from various sources to provide a holistic view of each customer. It uses AI and machine learning to analyze customer interactions and browsing behavior, enabling organizations to create personalized marketing campaigns. You can find out more information on Salesforce Customer 360 at salesforce.com.

Optimizing Inventory Management

Inventory management systems use AI to predict demand trends, ensuring optimal stock levels and reducing wastage. AI algorithms can analyze historical sales data, seasonal trends, and market conditions to forecast future demand accurately. This predictive capability allows retailers to maintain the right balance of stock, minimizing overstocking and stockouts.[lxix] Additionally, AI can optimize inventory replenishment by automating orders based on real-time sales data and inventory levels, ensuring that products are always available when customers need them.[lxx]

A couple of AI-driven inventory management platforms are:

- Zoho Inventory: It offers real-time tracking, automated workflows, and seamless integration with multiple sales channels. This tool is particularly useful for organizations looking to streamline their operations and reduce waste. You can find out more on the Zoho Inventory at zoho.com.
- Cin7: Excels in integration and demand forecasting and helps organizations manage their inventory across various platforms, ensuring that stock levels are optimized and sales opportunities are maximized. You can find out more information on Cin7 at cin7.com.

Improving Supply Chain Efficiency

In supply chain logistics, AI helps in route optimization and demand forecasting, streamlining operations from production to delivery. AI-powered systems can analyze various factors, such as traffic patterns, weather conditions, and delivery schedules, to determine the most efficient routes for transportation.[lxxi] This reduces fuel consumption, delivery times, and operational costs. Furthermore, AI-driven demand forecasting enables retailers to align their supply chain operations with market demand, reducing the risk of excess inventory and ensuring timely delivery of products to customers.[lxxii]

AI's integration into the retail industry is revolutionizing how organizations operate and interact with customers. By delivering personalized shopping experiences, optimizing inventory management, and enhancing supply chain efficiency, AI is driving significant improvements in customer satisfaction and operational excellence. As AI technologies continue to advance, they promise to further transform the retail landscape, enabling retailers to stay competitive, adapt to changing consumer preferences, and create more sustainable and efficient business models.

Manufacturing:

In the manufacturing sector, the integration of AI is transforming traditional processes and driving significant advancements in efficiency, productivity, and product quality. By leveraging AI for predictive maintenance, manufacturers can anticipate equipment failures before they occur, thus reducing downtime and minimizing costly disruptions. AI-powered quality control systems ensure that products meet stringent standards by detecting defects with unparalleled accuracy, thus leading to higher levels of consistency and customer satisfaction.

Furthermore, process automation enabled by AI optimizes production lines, streamlining operations and reducing human error. These innovations not only enhance overall performance but also enable manufacturers to remain competitive in a rapidly evolving industry. As AI technology continues to advance, its applications in manufacturing will undoubtedly expand, paving the way for even greater improvements and new opportunities in the sector.

Predictive Maintenance

Predictive maintenance uses AI to monitor equipment and predict failures before they occur, thereby minimizing downtime and maintenance costs. By analyzing data from sensors and other monitoring devices, AI algorithms can identify patterns and anomalies that indicate potential equipment failures. This allows manufacturers to perform maintenance only when needed rather than on a fixed schedule, which can lead to substantial cost savings and increased equipment lifespan.[lxxiii] For example, AI-driven predictive maintenance systems can detect early signs of wear and tear in machinery, enabling timely interventions that prevent costly breakdowns.[lxxiv]

A couple of AI-driven predictive maintenance platforms are:

C3.ai is an AI-based platform that helps organizations predict and prevent asset failures, offering comprehensive monitoring and proactive maintenance. You can find more information for C3.ai at c3.ai.

Dingo Trakka is another AI-based platform that specializes in asset health management. It combines data analytics and machine learning to optimize asset performance in heavy industries, such as mining and oil and gas. You can find more information about Dingo Trakka at dingo.com/solutions/trakka/.

Quality Control

AI-powered quality control systems can inspect products for defects with high precision while ensuring consistent quality. These systems use machine learning algorithms and computer vision technology to analyze images and sensor data, detecting defects that may be invisible to the human eye. By automating the inspection process, AI ensures that every product meets quality standards, reducing waste and enhancing customer satisfaction.[lxxv] An example is the use of AI in semiconductor manufacturing where AI systems can identify microscopic defects in silicon wafers, ensuring the reliability and performance of the final products.[lxxvi]

A couple of AI-driven quality control tools are:

- Saiwa's Fraime: It offers AI-powered tools such as anomaly detection, which is widely used in manufacturing for quality control. By identifying anomalies and deviations early in the production process, it enables manufacturers to proactively address potential defects, optimize workflows, and improve quality without the need for extensive in-house AI expertise. You can find out more information on Saiwa's Fraime at saiwa.ai.

- XenonStack: It provides AI-driven quality control solutions that utilize machine learning and deep learning models to analyze vast amounts of data, identify intricate patterns, and automate complex inspection tasks, helping to reduce defects, maximize productivity, and streamline production processes. You can find out more information on XenonStack at xenonstack.com.

Process Automation

Process automation driven by AI improves efficiency and productivity by automating repetitive tasks and optimizing production workflows. AI can optimize various aspects of the manufacturing process, from inventory management to production scheduling and workflow optimization. For example, AI algorithms can analyze production data to identify bottlenecks and suggest improvements, leading to more efficient use of resources and reduced production times.[lxxvii] Additionally, robotic process automation (RPA) can handle mundane and repetitive tasks such as assembly, packaging, and quality checks, freeing up human workers to focus on more complex and value-added activities.[lxxviii]

A couple of AI-enabled production scheduling platforms are:

- C3 AI Production Schedule Optimization: This platform helps production schedulers improve fill rates, line utilization, and profitability with dynamic production schedules. It unifies disparate data such as demand forecasts, sales orders, and inventory data, applying best-in-class optimization techniques to generate optimized schedules. You can find out more information on C3 AI Production Schedule Optimization at c3.ai.

- SkyPlanner APS: It's an automated software for production scheduling and finite capacity scheduling. It uses built-in AI to optimize the production of a factory in seconds, seamlessly integrating with enterprise resource planning and manufacturing execution systems to maintain optimal production levels while reacting to changes automatically. You can find out more information on SkyPlanner APS at skyplanner.ai.

A couple of AI-driven workflow optimization platforms are:

- CrewAI: An advanced AI agent framework that allows multiple AI agents to collaborate efficiently. It features multi-agent collaboration, task delegation, and API integrations. It's great for workflow automation and AI-powered customer service. You can find out more information on CrewAI at crewai.com.

- AutoGen: A platform designed to generate responses, automate processes, and optimize workflows. It supports autonomous agent execution, LLM integration, and API integration and is useful for content generation and customer support bots. You can find out more information on AutoGen at microsoft.com.

A couple of AI-driven robotic packaging systems are:

- Ranpak's Rabot: It utilizes a cutting-edge AI camera system to collect and analyze data at manual pack stations, providing actionable insights to optimize packing workflows, minimize material waste, and improve quality assurance. You can find out more about Ranpak's Rabot at ranpak.com.

- Pickle Robot: It specializes in AI-powered trailer unloading and packaging automation. Their robots use advanced AI and machine vision to handle various packaging tasks with precision and efficiency. You can find out more about Pickle Robot at picklerobot.com.

AI's integration into the manufacturing sector is driving remarkable improvements in efficiency, productivity, and product quality. By harnessing the power of predictive maintenance, AI helps prevent costly equipment failures and minimizes downtime, ensuring smooth and continuous operations. AI-powered quality control systems enhance product consistency and customer satisfaction by detecting defects with exceptional precision.[lxxix]

Additionally, process automation streamlines production lines, reducing human error and optimizing workflows. As AI technology continues to advance, its applications in manufacturing will expand even further, opening new avenues for innovation and competitive advantage.[lxxx]

Transportation:

The transportation industry is undergoing a remarkable transformation, primarily fueled by advancements in AI and related technologies. These innovations are revolutionizing how we move people and goods, enhancing safety, efficiency, and convenience across various modes of transportation. Autonomous vehicles are at the forefront of this revolution, with AI-powered systems enabling self-driving cars and trucks to navigate complex environments, reducing the risk of accidents and optimizing fuel consumption.

Additionally, AI-powered traffic management systems are improving urban mobility by analyzing real-time data to predict and alleviate congestion, leading to smoother and faster commutes. In the realm of logistics, AI is streamlining supply chain operations, enhancing route optimization, and ensuring timely deliveries.

Furthermore, public transportation is benefiting from AI through predictive maintenance, which minimizes downtime and ensures the reliability of services. As AI continues to evolve, its integration into the transportation sector promises to create a smarter, more connected world where travel is safer, more efficient, and more sustainable.

Autonomous Vehicles

Autonomous vehicles (AVs) represent one of the most revolutionary applications of AI in transportation. These vehicles utilize a combination of sensors, machine learning algorithms, and real-time data processing to navigate and make driving decisions autonomously. The safety benefits of AVs are profound as they have the potential to significantly reduce the number of accidents caused by human error, which accounts for approximately 94% of all traffic accidents.[lxxxi] By leveraging AI, AVs can also optimize routes in real-time, reducing traffic congestion and improving overall traffic flow.[lxxxii]

An example of Avs is Waymo, a company that develops self-driving cars. Waymo, a subsidiary of Alphabet Inc. (Google's parent company), has been testing and developing Avs in various locations, including Phoenix, Arizona. Their vehicles use a combination of sensors, cameras, and AI to navigate and drive without human intervention. They are designed to handle a range of driving scenarios, such as urban streets, highways, and complex intersections. They can detect and respond to other vehicles, pedestrians, cyclists, and various road conditions, all while ensuring passenger safety.[lxxxiii]

Traffic Management

AI-powered traffic management systems analyze vast amounts of real-time data from various sources, such as cameras, sensors, and GPS devices, to optimize traffic flow and reduce congestion. These systems can predict traffic patterns, adjust traffic signals dynamically, and provide real-time updates to commuters. By doing so, they help in minimizing delays and improving the efficiency of urban transportation networks.[lxxxiv] Moreover, the integration of AI in traffic management systems contributes to reduced fuel consumption and lower greenhouse gas emissions as vehicles spend less time idling and more time moving efficiently.[lxxxv]

A couple of AI-powered traffic management systems are:

- Google's AI Traffic Light System: It uses machine learning algorithms to optimize traffic flow by adjusting signal timings in real-time. It analyzes data from various sources, such as cameras and sensors, to predict traffic patterns and reduce congestion. You can find out more information about Google's AI Traffic Light System at sites.research.google/greenlight/.
- SCOOT: This system uses real-time data to dramatically adjust traffic signal timings, reducing delays by up to 20%. It integrates various components such as IoT sensors, cameras, and machine learning models to monitor and optimize traffic flow. You can learn more about SCOOT at mobility.siemens.com.

Logistics Optimization

In the logistics sector, AI enhances route planning and load optimization, leading to improved efficiency and reduced operational costs. AI algorithms can analyze historical data and real-time information to determine the most efficient delivery routes, taking into account factors such as traffic conditions, weather, and delivery windows.[lxxxvi] Additionally, AI can optimize load distribution in transportation vehicles, ensuring that space is utilized effectively and that the weight is evenly distributed to maintain vehicle stability.[lxxxvii] These advancements in logistics not only enhance the speed and reliability of deliveries but also contribute to a more sustainable transportation industry.[lxxxviii]

A couple of examples of AI-driven logistic platforms are:

- Blue Yonder Luminate: It uses AI and machine learning to create an autonomous supply chain, uncovering patterns and insights from real-time data for disruption prediction and automatic course correction. It also helps synchronize solutions across planning, execution, labor, e-commerce, and delivery, providing a single source of truth from planning through execution. You can find out more information on Blue Yonder's Luminate at blueyonder.com.

- Transmetrics: Offers AI-powered solutions for logistics planning and asset management. It connects with transportation management systems (TMS) and enterprise resource planning (ERP) software to optimize logistics strategies. It uses machine learning algorithms to improve data quality and provide historical reporting on operational performance. You can find out more information on Transmetrics at transmetrics.ai.

AI's integration into the transportation industry is revolutionizing how we move people and goods, making travel safer, more efficient, and more sustainable. With advancements in AVs, AI-driven traffic management systems, and optimized logistics, the transportation sector will achieve remarkable improvements in safety, convenience, and environmental impact. As AI continues to evolve, it will further enhance the connectivity and efficiency of transportation networks.

Marketing and Advertising:

AI is revolutionizing marketing and advertising by enabling more precise targeting, deeper customer insights, and enhanced campaign optimization. By analyzing vast amounts of data, AI algorithms can identify patterns and trends that were previously hidden, allowing marketers to tailor their strategies to individual customer preferences and behaviors. This level of precision in targeting ensures that marketing messages reach the right audience at the right time, increasing the effectiveness of campaigns and maximizing return on investment (ROI).

Additionally, AI-powered tools can provide real-time analytics and feedback, enabling marketers to adjust and optimize their campaigns on the fly. This dynamic approach not only enhances the overall efficiency of marketing efforts but also fosters a more personalized and engaging experience for customers.

Traditional marketing approaches often relied on broad demographic data and intuition, which could lead to inefficiencies and misallocated resources. AI, on the other hand, leverages vast amounts of data to create highly detailed consumer profiles, allowing for more accurate targeting of advertisements. This precision increases the likelihood of reaching potential customers who are genuinely interested in the products or services being advertised, thereby enhancing engagement and conversion rates.[lxxxix]

AI analyzes consumer behavior to deliver highly targeted advertisements, increasing relevance and engagement. By analyzing browsing history, purchase patterns, and social media activity, AI can identify trends and preferences at an individual level. For example, machine learning algorithms can predict what products a user is likely to buy next based on their past behavior. This allows marketers to deliver personalized advertisements that resonate with consumers, making them more likely to respond positively.[xc]

A couple of AI-powered platforms that analyze consumer behavior to deliver targeted advertisements are:

- Quantilope: An AI tool that provides deep insights into consumer behavior. It offers automated research solutions that help organizations understand their customers' needs and preferences. Its AI-driven platform can analyze qualitative data at scale, making it easier for organizations to tailor their strategies and products to meet customer expectations. You can find out more about Quantilope at ourcrowd.com.

- Qualtrics: Offers a comprehensive suite of tools for market research, customer experience, and employee engagement. It leverages advanced AI and machine learning algorithms to analyze data and provide actionable insights. You can find out more information about Qualtrics at qualtrics.com.

Customer insights derived from AI help executives understand preferences and trends. AI-driven analytics tools can process large volumes of data from various sources to extract valuable insights about customer behavior. These insights can reveal which products are gaining popularity, how consumer preferences are shifting over time, and what factors influence purchasing decisions. Executives can use this information to tailor their marketing strategies to better meet the needs and desires of their target audience.[xci]

AI-powered tools optimize campaign performance by adjusting parameters in real-time based on data analysis, maximizing return on investment for an organization utilizing the tools. Unlike traditional marketing campaigns that require extensive planning and manual adjustments, AI-enabled systems can automatically adjust campaign parameters such as ad placement, budget allocation, and audience targeting in real-time. These adjustments are based on continuous data analysis, ensuring that marketing efforts remain effective and efficient. As a result, executives can achieve higher returns on their marketing investments by minimizing waste and maximizing the impact of their campaigns.[xcii]

AI is profoundly transforming marketing and advertising by enabling more precise targeting, deeper customer insights, and optimized campaign strategies. By harnessing the power of AI, marketers can deliver highly personalized and relevant content, increasing engagement and driving better results. AI-driven analytics and real-time feedback allow for continuous improvement and adaptation of marketing efforts, ensuring that campaigns remain effective and aligned with customer needs.

Human Resources:

Human resources departments are also harnessing AI to revolutionize the way they operate, streamlining recruitment processes, enhancing employee engagement, and efficiently managing the workforce. AI-powered tools are transforming recruitment by automating candidate screening, enabling HR professionals to identify the best talent quickly and accurately. These tools analyze resumes, assess candidate fit based on predefined criteria, and even conduct initial interviews, saving time and reducing bias in the hiring process. In terms of employee engagement, AI-driven platforms provide personalized feedback, recognize achievements, and suggest professional development opportunities, fostering a more motivated and productive workforce.

Additionally, AI is optimizing workforce management by predicting staffing needs, managing employee schedules, and analyzing performance data to identify areas for improvement. As AI continues to advance, its integration into human resources promises to create more efficient, fair, and responsive HR practices, ultimately enhancing the overall employee experience and organizational effectiveness.

A couple of AI-enabled platforms that optimize workflow management are:

- AllVoices: This AI-driven platform goes beyond collecting feedback by transforming each report into a structured case, giving teams a clear path to investigate and resolve issues. It provides real-time insights into workplace concerns and helps tackle root causes, leading to a healthier and more responsive organizational culture. For more information, you can check out AllVoices at allvoices.co.

- Opmed's Staff Scheduling Optimizer: This AI-powered platform does more than basic shift management by optimizing every detail to ensure all teams work at peak efficiency. It aligns staff skills and availability with real-time operational needs, reducing costly overtime and reliance on agency staff. For more information, you can check out Opmed's Staff Scheduling Optimizer at opmed.ai.

Traditionally, HR tasks such as recruitment, employee engagement, and workforce management require extensive manual effort and time. AI is transforming these functions by automating repetitive tasks and providing data-driven insights, thereby increasing efficiency and effectiveness in HR practices.[xciii]

A couple of AI-driven recruitment platforms are:

- Iris by Queros: This platform automates the sourcing, shortlisting, and outreaches to candidates in just 24 seconds. It helps recruiters and hiring managers discover profiles and match them with relevant candidates. Iris generates customized job descriptions to attract the right talent and sends hyper-personalized messages to shortlisted candidates. You can learn more about Iris by Queros at queoros.com.

- Elevatus: This recruitment software automates the entire talent acquisition cycle, from creating job requisitions to onboarding new hires. It helps organizations streamline core functions such as posting jobs, shortlisting top talent, interviewing candidates, evaluating top performers, managing visas, accepting advanced analytics, running background checks, inviting recruitment agencies, and onboarding new hires. You can check out Elevatus at elevates.io.

AI-driven recruitment platforms analyze resumes and assess candidates, identifying the best fit for roles with greater accuracy and efficiency. Recruitment is a critical function in HR, and finding the right candidate can be a complex and time-consuming process. AI-powered platforms can rapidly scan and analyze large volumes of resumes, looking for specific keywords and qualifications that match job requirements. These platforms use machine learning algorithms to assess candidate fit based on skills, experience, and other factors, significantly improving the accuracy and speed of the hiring process.[xciv]

Employee engagement tools use AI to monitor sentiment and provide insights into employee satisfaction and retention. Employee engagement is essential for organizational success, as engaged employees are more productive and less likely to leave. AI-driven tools can analyze employee communication, surveys, and social media interactions to gauge sentiment and identify potential issues affecting morale. These insights enable HR professionals to proactively address concerns and implement strategies to enhance employee satisfaction and retention.[xcv]

A couple of AI-powered platforms that measure employee sentiment are:

- CultureMonkey: An AI-driven platform designed to measure and improve employee sentiment. It uses advanced sentiment analysis algorithms to interpret employee feedback from surveys, emails, and other communication channels. It provides real-time insights into employee emotions, helping organizations identify areas of concern and take proactive measures to enhance workplace culture. You can find more information on CultureMonkey at culturemonkey.io.
- Effy AI: A powerful tool that leverages AI to analyze employee sentiment. It offers features like AI-generated performance reviews and sentiment analysis of employee feedback. It also provides actionable insights into employee satisfaction and engagement, enabling HR teams to address issues promptly and foster a positive work environment. You can find more information on Effy AI at effy.ai.

Workforce management systems leverage AI to optimize scheduling, performance evaluation, and talent development. Effective workforce management involves scheduling, performance monitoring, and ongoing development of employees. AI systems can optimize scheduling by predicting workforce needs based on historical data and real-time information. Additionally, AI can enhance performance evaluations by providing objective, data-driven assessments of employee performance, reducing biases. For talent development, AI can identify skill gaps and recommend personalized training programs, ensuring employees continue to grow and contribute to the organization.[xcvi]

A couple of AI-driven workforce management platforms are:

- WorkFusion: An AI-powered platform that specializes in intelligent automation for workforce management. It combines robotic process automation (RPA) with AI-driven analytics to automate repetitive tasks, manage workflows, and optimize workforce productivity. It helps organizations reduce operational costs and improve efficiency by leveraging AI to monitor and manage workforce activities. You can find out more information on WorkFusion at workfusion.com.

- Deputy: An AI-enabled workforce management platform that focuses on employee scheduling, time tracking, and task management. It uses AI algorithms to predict staffing needs, optimize shift schedules, and ensure compliance with labor laws. Deputy's intuitive interface and real-time analytics provide insights into employee performance and help managers make data-driven decisions. You can find out more information on Deputy at deputy.com.

The integration of AI into human resources is revolutionizing the way organizations attract, engage, and manage their workforce. By automating recruitment processes, enhancing employee engagement through personalized feedback and development opportunities, and optimizing workforce management, AI is creating more efficient and effective HR practices. These advancements not only save time and reduce bias but also foster a more motivated and productive workforce.

AI's transformative impact is already starting to revolutionize industries across the board, from healthcare and finance to retail, manufacturing, transportation, marketing, and human resources. By automating processes, enhancing decision-making, and driving unprecedented levels of efficiency and innovation, AI is reshaping the way they operate and interact with their customers. As AI technology continues to evolve, its applications will expand even further, offering new opportunities for growth and innovation.

Chapter 4:
Case Studies Of Successful AI Implementations

Examining case studies of successful AI implementations reveals the incredible power of AI technologies across diverse industries. Organizations are leveraging AI to drive innovation, enhance efficiency, and achieve significant business outcomes.

In healthcare, AI-powered diagnostic tools are enabling earlier detection of diseases and personalized treatment plans, improving patient outcomes. In finance, AI algorithms are optimizing investment strategies and detecting fraudulent activities, ensuring the security and integrity of financial transactions. Retailers are using AI to personalize customer experiences and optimize inventory management, leading to increased customer satisfaction and operational efficiency. Manufacturers are leveraging AI for predictive maintenance and process automation, boosting productivity and product quality. The transportation sector is benefiting from AI-driven traffic management and autonomous vehicles, enhancing safety and reducing congestion.

A review of specific case studies will demonstrate that AI is not just a futuristic concept but a practical tool revolutionizing industries and driving tangible results today.

Case Study: AI-Driven Diagnostic Tools in Healthcare

A notable example in healthcare is the deployment of AI-driven diagnostic tools in hospitals. These tools use machine learning algorithms to analyze medical images such as X-rays and MRIs, identifying anomalies with higher accuracy than human radiologists. The integration of AI into diagnostic procedures has marked a significant improvement in the accuracy and efficiency of medical imaging analysis. By training on vast datasets of annotated medical images, AI algorithms can learn to recognize patterns and anomalies that might be too subtle or complex for human radiologists to detect reliably. This capability has been particularly beneficial in the early detection of diseases such as cancer, where early intervention can significantly improve patient outcomes.[xcvii]

At the Cleveland Clinic, an AI-powered tool was integrated into their radiology department's workflow. This system, designed to assist with the interpretation of chest X-rays, was able to identify potential issues such as lung nodules, fractures, and other critical findings with remarkable accuracy. The tool's deployment led to a notable decrease in diagnostic errors, with the error rate dropping by

30% within the first year of implementation. Furthermore, the early detection of serious conditions allowed for timely treatment, thereby improving overall patient care and outcomes.[xcviii]

This case study illustrates the transformative impact AI-driven diagnostic tools can have on healthcare, demonstrating how technology can enhance accuracy, reduce errors, and ultimately improve patient outcomes.

Case Study: AI Integration in Finance

In the finance industry, a major bank has successfully integrated AI into its fraud detection system. The integration of AI into fraud detection systems has transformed how banks handle potential fraudulent activities. These AI systems utilize machine learning algorithms to analyze vast amounts of transaction data in real time, identifying patterns and anomalies that may indicate fraudulent behavior.[xcix]

The AI algorithms analyze transaction data in real time, identifying suspicious activities and flagging potential fraud cases. These algorithms are trained on historical transaction data, learning to distinguish between normal and suspicious activities. They consider various factors such as transaction amount, device used, frequency, and location. When a transaction deviates significantly from established patterns, the system flags it for further investigation.

This real-time analysis allows for immediate responses to potential fraud, preventing unauthorized transactions before they can cause significant harm.[c]

One notable implementation of AI-driven fraud detection was at JPMorgan Chase, where the adoption of AI systems led to a marked improvement in detecting fraudulent activities. The bank reported a substantial reduction in false positives, which are legitimate transactions incorrectly flagged as fraud. This reduction not only improved operational efficiency by reducing the number of manual reviews required but also enhanced the customer experience by minimizing disruptions. The accuracy of fraud detection was also significantly improved, providing better protection for both the bank and its customers.[ci]

This case study demonstrates the significant impact of AI on enhancing fraud detection in the finance industry and showcases how technology can provide real-time protection and improve overall security measures.

Case Study: Personalized Marketing in Retail

A global retail giant has leveraged AI to enhance customer experience through personalized marketing. In the highly competitive retail industry, companies are increasingly turning to AI to gain an edge by providing more personalized and engaging experiences for their customers. AI technologies enable retailers to go beyond traditional market segmentation (dividing the overall market into distinct groups of consumers who have similar needs, characteristics, or behaviors) and offer truly individualized interactions.[cii]

The AI system analyzes customer behavior, purchase history, and preferences to deliver tailored product recommendations and promotions. By analyzing vast amounts of data on customer behavior, including browsing patterns, purchase history, and product preferences, AI systems can identify trends and preferences unique to each customer. This analysis allows retailers to deliver personalized product recommendations and promotions that are more likely to resonate with individual customers. For example, if a customer frequently purchases athletic gear, the AI system can suggest new arrivals in sportswear or offer special discounts on fitness-related products.[ciii]

One prominent example is Amazon, which has successfully implemented AI-driven personalized marketing strategies to enhance customer experience. By leveraging machine learning algorithms, Amazon can predict what products customers are likely to be interested in and offer personalized recommendations on its website and through targeted emails. This personalized approach has resulted in a significant boost in sales and improved customer retention rates. Specifically, Amazon reported a 20% increase in sales and a 15% improvement in customer retention due to its personalized marketing efforts.[civ]

This case study illustrates the powerful impact AI can have on enhancing customer experience and driving business growth in the retail industry through personalized marketing.

Case Study: Predictive Maintenance in Manufacturing

An automotive manufacturer has implemented AI for predictive maintenance on its assembly line. In the manufacturing sector, predictive maintenance has become a game-changer, particularly in industries with complex and high-value equipment. By leveraging AI technologies, companies can monitor the health and performance of machinery in real time, identifying potential issues before they lead to costly breakdowns.[cv]

The AI system monitors equipment performance and predicts potential failures, allowing maintenance to be scheduled proactively. Predictive maintenance systems use a variety of sensors to collect data on machine conditions such as temperature, vibration, and pressure. Machine learning algorithms then analyze this data to detect patterns indicative of potential failures. For example, an increase in vibration might signal that a component is nearing the end of its life. By predicting these failures, the system allows maintenance teams to address issues proactively, scheduling repairs during planned downtime rather than reacting to unexpected breakdowns.[cvi]

A case study from General Motors illustrates the benefits of AI-driven predictive maintenance. The implementation of an AI system on their assembly line led to a 25% reduction in unplanned downtime. This improvement was achieved by accurately predicting failures and scheduling maintenance at optimal times, thus minimizing disruptions to production. Additionally, the proactive approach to maintenance resulted in a significant decrease in overall maintenance costs, as it prevented severe damage to equipment that would have required more extensive and expensive repairs with significant downtime.[cvii]

This case study highlights the major impact of AI on predictive maintenance in manufacturing, showcasing the notable improvements in operational efficiency and cost savings.

Case Study: AI-Powered Traffic Management in Transportation

A city has deployed an AI-powered traffic management system to address congestion and improve public transportation efficiency. Urban areas around the world are encountering increasing traffic congestion, leading to longer commute times, higher fuel consumption, and elevated emissions. To tackle these challenges, many cities are turning to AI to optimize traffic flow and enhance the efficiency of their transportation systems.[cviii]

The AI-driven system analyzes real-time traffic data and adjusts traffic signal timings to optimize flow. These systems collect data from various sources, including traffic cameras, sensors, and GPS devices. Machine learning algorithms then analyze this data in real time to identify traffic patterns and congestion points. By dynamically adjusting traffic signal timings, they are able to optimize the flow of vehicles through intersections, reducing stop-and-go traffic and improving overall traffic efficiency.[cix]

An example of successful implementation is the use of the SURTRAC (Scalable Urban Traffic Control) system in Pittsburgh, Pennsylvania. This AI-driven system uses real-time data to adjust traffic signals at key intersections. The deployment of SURTRAC led to a 15% reduction in travel times, as well as a 10% decrease in fuel consumption due to smoother traffic flow and fewer stops. These improvements not only enhance commuter experiences but also contribute to environmental sustainability by lowering vehicle emissions.[cx]

This case study highlights the significant benefits of AI in improving traffic management and reducing urban congestion, demonstrating one-way how intelligent systems can make cities more efficient and sustainable.

Case Study: AI-Driven Marketing Campaigns

A technology company has achieved remarkable success with AI-driven marketing campaigns. By analyzing customer data and behavior, the AI system segments the audience and targets them with personalized messages. The integration of AI into marketing strategies allows organizations to leverage vast amounts of data to gain deeper insights into customer behavior and preferences. This technology enables more precise market segmentation, ensuring that marketing messages are tailored to the unique needs and interests of different customer groups.[cxi]

An exemplary case is the use of AI in marketing by Salesforce. The company implemented an AI-driven platform known as Einstein, which analyzes customer data from various channels, such as emails, social media interactions, and purchasing history. By applying machine learning algorithms, the platform segments the audience and predicts which messages are most likely to resonate with each segment. The personalized approach resulted in a 30% increase in engagement rates and significantly enhanced the overall effectiveness of marketing campaigns. Since customers received relevant content that aligned with their preferences, it led to higher interaction and conversion rates.[cxii]

This case study demonstrates the powerful impact of AI-driven marketing on enhancing engagement and effectiveness, illustrating how tailored messaging can lead to significant improvements in campaign outcomes.

Case Study: AI in HR for Recruitment and Employee Engagement

An organization has streamlined its recruitment process by using an AI-driven platform to screen resumes and conduct initial candidate assessments. The traditional recruitment process often involves manual screening of resumes, which can be time-consuming and prone to bias. By integrating AI into the recruitment process, organizations can automate the initial stages of candidate screening and significantly improve efficiency and consistency.[cxiii]

For example, Unilever implemented an AI-driven recruitment platform that utilizes machine learning algorithms to assess resumes and conduct initial candidate assessments through digital interviews. This system analyzes various factors, such as skills, experience, and behavioral traits, to identify the best-fit candidates for each role. As a result, Unilever experienced a 40% reduction in time-to-hire and a marked improvement in the quality of new hires, as evidenced by better alignment with job requirements and higher performance levels.[cxiv]

Additionally, AI-powered employee engagement tools have provided insights into workforce satisfaction, leading to more effective retention strategies. Employee engagement is critical to maintaining a motivated and productive workforce. AI-powered tools can monitor employee sentiment by analyzing communication patterns, survey responses, and other data sources.

For example, an AI-enabled platform at IBM analyzes employee feedback to identify trends and potential issues affecting morale. These insights enable HR professionals to develop targeted retention strategies, addressing concerns proactively and enhancing overall employee satisfaction and retention.[cxv]

These case studies illustrate how AI can significantly enhance both recruitment efficiency and employee engagement, thereby leading to improved hiring quality and workforce satisfaction.

In today's business world, the AI revolution is not just an innovation; it's reshaping industries, redefining possibilities, and setting the stage for a future where the synergy between human ingenuity and AI will drive unprecedented growth and success for organizations. These case studies highlight the potential of AI in driving innovation, enhancing efficiency, and achieving substantial business outcomes. They also demonstrate that AI is not merely a theoretical concept but a practical and powerful tool that executives can now leverage to solve complex challenges, optimize operations, and unlock new opportunities.

As AI continues to evolve and mature, its impact will only grow, paving the way for even more groundbreaking applications and success stories.

Chapter 5:
AI In Decision-Making

In this chapter, we look into the transformative potential of AI in revolutionizing executive decision-making. By harnessing the power of AI, executives are able to make more informed and accurate decisions. AI's predictive analytics capabilities allow executives to forecast trends and outcomes with greater precision, facilitating proactive planning and strategic initiatives.

AI-driven risk management tools also help identify and mitigate potential threats, ensuring a more secure and resilient operation. Moreover, AI supports strategic planning by providing a comprehensive analysis and actionable recommendations, empowering executives to steer their organizations toward sustained growth and success.

How AI Can Support Executive Decision-Making

Leveraging AI for executive decision-making empowers leaders with data-driven insights, predictive analytics, and actionable intelligence, thereby enhancing their ability to make informed, strategic choices.

Data-Driven Insights

AI can process and analyze vast amounts of data quickly, providing executives with valuable insights that might be overlooked by human analysts. For example, AI systems can analyze transactional data to identify purchasing patterns, customer demographics, and seasonal trends. A retail company could use these insights to tailor marketing campaigns, optimize inventory, and improve customer satisfaction. AI can also integrate data from multiple sources, such as social media, customer feedback, and sales records, to create a comprehensive view of market dynamics. This holistic approach enables executives to make informed decisions based on empirical evidence rather than intuition alone.[cxvi]

Predictive Analytics

Predictive analytics uses AI to forecast future trends and outcomes by analyzing historical data. For example, an AI model can predict sales trends by examining past performance data, seasonal variations, and market conditions. By incorporating external factors such as economic indicators, competitor actions, and consumer sentiment, AI models can provide more accurate and reliable forecasts. This foresight allows executives to anticipate changes, allocate resources more effectively, and devise strategies to capitalize on upcoming opportunities. For example, a retailer can use predictive analytics to forecast demand for different products and optimize inventory levels, reducing costs and improving customer satisfaction.[cxvii]

Risk Management

AI can play a crucial role in risk management by analyzing potential scenarios and their impacts. AI models can assess various risk factors, such as market volatility, regulatory changes, and operational disruptions, providing executives with a comprehensive risk profile. For example, in the financial industry, AI can analyze market trends, historical data, and geopolitical events to identify potential risks to investment portfolios. This proactive approach helps in mitigating risks and making contingency plans. Additionally, AI can monitor real-time data and alert executives to emerging risks, allowing for timely intervention and response.[cxviii]

Operational Efficiency

AI can optimize organizational processes and resource allocation, leading to improved operational efficiency. For example, AI-driven automation can streamline repetitive tasks, reducing the burden on employees and minimizing errors. AI can also analyze production data to identify inefficiencies and recommend process improvements. For example, in manufacturing, AI can monitor machinery performance, predict maintenance needs, and optimize production schedules to reduce downtime and enhance productivity. Moreover, AI can analyze supply chain data to identify bottlenecks and optimize logistics, leading to faster and more efficient operations.[cxix]

Real-Time Decision Support

In critical decision-making moments, AI can provide executives with real-time information and recommendations. For example, during a crisis, an AI system can analyze data from various sources, such as social media, news outlets, and internal reports, to offer a comprehensive situational overview. When identifying relevant information, it can filter out noise and provide actionable insights to help executives make informed decisions quickly. This enables executives to respond swiftly and effectively, minimizing the impact of the crisis. For example, during a natural disaster, AI can analyze weather data, transportation routes, and supply chain information to help executives coordinate emergency response efforts.[cxx]

Strategic Planning

AI can enhance long-term strategic planning by simulating different scenarios and their potential outcomes. Executives can use AI to test various strategies, assess their feasibility, and identify the best course of action. For example, AI can model the impact of market entry into a new region, considering factors such as consumer behavior, competitor presence, and regulatory environment. By simulating different scenarios, it can help executives identify potential risks and opportunities, enabling them to make data-driven strategic decisions. This data-driven approach ensures that strategic decisions are well-informed and aligned with organizational goals, thereby reducing the likelihood of costly mistakes and improving overall business performance.[cxxi]

Personalized Recommendations

AI-driven personalized advice and strategies can be tailored to an executive's specific needs and objectives. For example, AI can analyze an executive's past decisions, preferences, and performance metrics to provide customized recommendations for future actions. This personalized approach enhances decision-making and supports individual growth. For example, AI can analyze an executive's leadership style, communication patterns, and decision-making history to offer tailored advice on improving team collaboration and achieving organizational goals. Furthermore, it can provide personalized training and development plans, helping executives build the skills and knowledge needed for effective leadership.[cxxii]

Enhanced Competitive Intelligence

AI can monitor competitors and market conditions to provide executives with valuable insights for informed strategic decisions.

By analyzing competitors' activities, market trends, and consumer sentiments can help executives identify opportunities and threats, enabling them to stay ahead of the competition. For example, AI can analyze social media data, news articles, and financial reports to monitor competitor strategies and market movements. This information can then be used to inform product development, marketing campaigns, and organizational expansion plans. Additionally, AI can identify emerging trends and consumer preferences, helping executives stay ahead of market changes and make proactive decisions.[cxxiii]

As AI continues to evolve and integrate into decision-making processes, it will not only streamline organizational operations but will also pave the way for a future where informed and intelligent choices become the cornerstone of organizational success.

Effective Engineering Prompts

Generative AI models like ChatGPT, Perplexity, CoPilot, and others have revolutionized how humans interact with AI. These tools thrive on their ability to generate human-like text, craft creative content, and solve complex problems—powered by the prompts they receive. At the heart of maximizing these capabilities lies the art and science of prompt engineering. This process involves crafting well-designed inputs to guide AI models to produce accurate, relevant, and contextually appropriate outputs. Below is a comprehensive exploration of effective prompt engineering and its role in harnessing generative AI's full potential.[cxxiv]

Understanding the Basics of Prompt Engineering:

Generative AI models rely on input prompts to generate text. A prompt is essentially the instruction or query that you give to the model, acting as its guide or framework. The quality of the output directly correlates with the clarity, specificity, and structure of the prompt. Poorly designed prompts often result in generic, irrelevant, or incoherent responses. On the other hand, well-crafted prompts enable users to extract meaningful and actionable insights from the model. Therefore, the key lies in understanding the nuances of creating prompts that balance precision, flexibility, and depth.[cxxv]

The following are the key characteristics of effective generative AI prompting.

1. Clarity and Specificity:

A prompt should clearly articulate what the AI should produce as vague or ambiguous instructions leave room for misinterpretation.[cxxvi]

For example:

- Vague Prompt: "Explain technology."
- Effective Prompt: "Describe the applications of blockchain technology in supply chain management."

2. Contextual Framing:

Including context in the prompt helps the AI understand the background or scope of the task. This is particularly important when working on complex or multi-layered queries.[cxxvii] For example:

- Without Context: "Summarize this."
- With Context: "Summarize this technical research paper for a general audience."

3. Defining Output Format:

Specifying the structure or format of the desired output will help ensure that the result aligns with the desired format.[cxxviii] For example:

- General Prompt: "List advantages of renewable energy."
- Enhanced Prompt: "Provide a bullet-point list of five key advantages of renewable energy, with each point explained in one sentence."

4. Purpose Orientation:

By aligning the prompt with the end goal, it ensures you actionable and more favorable outputs.[cxxix] For example:

- Generic Prompt: "Write about cybersecurity."
- Purposeful Prompt: "Draft a one-page executive summary on how small businesses can protect themselves against phishing attacks."

5. Incorporating Role or Perspective:

By assigning the AI a role, it can help guide the tone and voice of the output.[cxxx] For example:

- Prompt: "Act as a marketing consultant and write a pitch for a new eco-friendly product."

Specific Prompt Engineering Techniques:

The following are specific prompt engineering techniques to become a better prompt writer and ultimately lead to the kind of outputs desired.

1. **Iteration and Refinement:**

Start with a basic prompt and then refine it based on the initial outputs as iterative adjustments help to optimize the results.[cxxxi] For example:

- Initial Prompt: "Explain cloud computing."
- Refined Prompt: "Explain cloud computing for high school students, using analogies to make the concept easy to understand."

2. **Experimenting with Styles:**

Try to leverage diverse tones and styles depending on the context. Whether drafting formal reports, casual posts, or creative stories, tailoring the prompt can make a substantial difference.[cxxxii] For example:

- Prompt: "Write a persuasive essay on the importance of AI ethics."

3. **Using Constraints:**

By adding constraints in prompts like word limits, specific formats, or keywords, for example, can help target the output more effectively.[cxxxiii]

For example:

- Prompt: "Provide a 150-word summary of the benefits of remote work, emphasizing productivity and flexibility."

4. Zero-Shot vs. Few-Shot Learning:

Zero-Shot Prompting: Provide minimal input, and then rely on the AI's inherent training to generate responses.[cxxxiv] For example:

- Prompt: "Translate 'Good morning' to French."

Few-Shot Prompting: Provide examples or a pattern for the AI to follow.[cxxxv] For example:

Translate these phrases to French:
- Hello: Bonjour
- Thank you: Merci
- Good morning: [Output expected here]

5. Prompt Chaining:

For complex tasks, try to break down the prompts into a series of smaller, interconnected instructions to achieve better results.[cxxxvi] For example:

- Step 1: "List the major themes of the novel '1984.'"

- Step 2: "Explain each theme briefly in two sentences."

Tip: Record the effective prompts that yield the desired results as this will help foster consistent outcomes and enable future replication or improvement of similar tasks.

Ethical Considerations in Prompt Engineering:

Effective prompt engineering isn't only about technical mastery— it's also about ethical responsibility. Be sure to consider the following principles when crafting prompts:

1. Avoid Bias and Stereotypes:

Try to design prompts that steer clear of promoting harmful biases or stereotypes in the model's outputs as this ensures that AI-generated content aligns with ethical guidelines and contributes to fostering inclusivity, fairness, and respect in communication. This approach helps to avoid reinforcing societal prejudices and builds trust in the responsible use of AI technology.[cxxxvii]

2. Promote Transparency:

When using AI-generated content in professional contexts, be sure to be transparent about its origins as this promotes ethical practices and allows others to assess the credibility and reliability of the information. Transparency also builds trust and fosters accountability when incorporating AI-generated content.

3. Encourage Fact-Checking:

Even with the most meticulously and carefully designed prompts, AI outputs often include inaccuracies. As such, always validate that the factual information provided is in fact accurate.[cxxxviii]

Examples of Prompts for Different Business Uses:

The following are just a few of the many examples of how to use generative AI models as a virtual assistant for you.

1. Business and Strategy:

- "Draft a proposal outlining the benefits of using AI in customer service operations, including the cost savings and efficiency improvements for the organization."

2. Learning:

- "Explain in two paragraphs what quantum computing is for non-experts and how it works."

3. Technical Documentation:

- "Summarize the latest advancements in quantum computing for non-experts, in three paragraphs."

4. Image Creation:

- "Generate a high resolution image that for a social media marketing campaign that depicts quantum computing and specifically states Smarter than Ever and it must state all of these words and be spelled exactly as written."

Mastering the art of prompt engineering empowers executives to unlock the full potential of generative AI models. It's not merely a technical skill, but also a creative endeavor—requiring a blend of clear communication, strategic thinking, and iterative experimentation. As generative AI continues to advance, the ability to craft effective prompts will remain a cornerstone of meaningful, impactful, and responsible AI usage.

Chapter 6:
AI For Operational Efficiency

In this chapter, we will explore how harnessing the power of AI can significantly enhance operational efficiency within organizations. By leveraging advanced data analytics, automation, and predictive modeling, AI enables executives to streamline processes, reduce costs, and boost overall productivity. AI-driven data analytics provide valuable insights into operational performance, identifying areas for improvement and optimizing resource allocation. Automation of routine tasks reduces human error and frees up employees to focus on more strategic initiatives. Predictive modeling anticipates future trends and demands, allowing executives to proactively adjust their operations and stay ahead of the competition. As we examine these applications, we will uncover the potential of AI in driving operational excellence and achieving sustainable growth for organizations.

Streamlining Organizational Processes with AI

Leveraging AI to streamline organizational processes revolutionizes traditional workflows, enhancing efficiency, accuracy, and agility through automation, predictive analytics, and data-driven decision-making.

Automation of Routine Tasks

Utilize the power of AI to automate routine tasks as this significantly enhances efficiency, reduces human error, and frees up valuable resources for more strategic and creative organizational endeavors. To effectively identify repetitive tasks, executives can use process mining tools that analyze event logs from various systems to pinpoint tasks that are repetitive and time-consuming. Some popular process mining tools include Celonis, IBM Process Mining, UiPath, and Fluxicon Disco. For example, in healthcare, process mining can identify repetitive data entry tasks in patient record management, which can then be automated to reduce the administrative burden on healthcare providers.[cxxxix]

AI-powered robotic process automation (RPA) can go beyond simple rule-based automation by incorporating machine learning to handle unstructured data and make more complex decisions. For example, in customer service, AI-powered RPA can analyze customer emails to extract relevant information, generate responses, and route more complex queries to human agents. This not only improves efficiency but also enhances the customer experience by providing faster and more accurate responses.[cxl]

Optimizing Workflow Management

Optimize workflow management with AI to enable more efficient coordination, real-time monitoring, and intelligent decision-making, ultimately enhancing productivity and reducing operational bottlenecks.

Advanced AI tools can create digital twins of workflows, allowing executives to simulate different scenarios and identify the most efficient processes. For example, in logistics, a digital twin of the supply chain can help identify bottlenecks, optimize inventory levels, and reduce delivery times. By continuously monitoring and analyzing these digital twins, executives can adapt to changes in demand and external factors while ensuring optimal performance.[cxli]

AI-driven project management tools can provide real-time insights into project progress, resource utilization, and potential risks. For example, a construction company might use AI to analyze project schedules, detect potential delays due to weather conditions, and suggest reallocating resources to stay on track. These tools can also facilitate better communication and collaboration by providing a centralized platform where team members can share updates, documents, and feedback.[cxlii]

AI-powered collaboration platforms can integrate with other tools and systems to provide a seamless communication experience. For example, an AI assistant in a platform like Microsoft Teams can automatically generate meeting minutes, assign action items, and remind team members of upcoming deadlines. By leveraging natural language processing (NLP), these assistants can understand and respond to queries, making it easier for teams to access the information they need quickly.[cxliii]

Enhancing Decision-Making

Leveraging AI to enhance executive decision-making processes in organizations has revolutionized the way data is analyzed, providing deeper insights, predictive analytics, and data-driven strategies that empower executives to make informed and timely decisions.

AI-powered decision support systems can process and analyze real-time data from multiple sources, providing actionable insights and recommendations. For example, in retail, AI can analyze sales data, customer behavior, and external factors like weather patterns to optimize pricing strategies and promotions. These systems can also detect anomalies, such as sudden drops in sales, and provide recommendations to address the issue promptly.[cxliv]

Predictive analytics can help executives anticipate future trends and make proactive decisions. For example, in the automotive industry, predictive analytics can forecast demand for specific car models, enabling manufacturers to adjust production schedules and supply chain operations accordingly. In healthcare, predictive analytics can identify patients at risk of chronic conditions, allowing for early intervention and personalized care plans.[cxlv]

AI can continuously monitor organizational processes, using machine learning algorithms to identify patterns and inefficiencies. For example, in finance, AI can analyze transaction data to detect inefficiencies in payment processing and recommend improvements to reduce costs and enhance security. By continuously learning from data, AI can adapt to changes in the business environment and provide ongoing recommendations for process optimization.[cxlvi]

Improving Customer Service

Using AI to improve customer service has changed the way organizations interact with their customers, providing personalized experiences, rapid response times, and efficient resolution of inquiries, thus enhancing overall customer satisfaction and loyalty.

AI chatbots and virtual assistants can be integrated with customer relationship management (CRM) systems to provide personalized support based on customer history and preferences. CRM systems are software applications designed to help executives manage and analyze interactions with current and potential customers. For example, an AI chatbot on an e-commerce website can assist customers with product recommendations, order tracking, and returns, providing a seamless shopping experience. By leveraging natural language processing (NLP), these chatbots can understand and respond to customer inquiries in a conversational manner, improving satisfaction.[cxlvii]

AI can analyze vast amounts of customer data to provide highly personalized experiences. For example, in the hospitality industry, AI can analyze guest preferences and behaviors to provide personalized recommendations for room amenities, dining options, and activities. By offering tailored experiences, organizations can increase customer loyalty and drive repeat business.[cxlviii]

AI can streamline customer support processes by automating routine tasks and triaging more complex queries to human agents. For example, in the telecommunications industry, AI can handle common customer inquiries about billing and technical support, reducing response times and freeing up human agents to address more complex issues. By providing quick and accurate responses, AI can enhance customer satisfaction and improve overall service quality.[cxlix]

Thus, embracing AI for operational efficiency is no longer a futuristic concept but a present-day necessity. By integrating AI-driven solutions, executives can streamline processes, enhance accuracy, and optimize resource allocation. From automating routine tasks to providing data-driven insights, AI empowers organizations to operate more effectively and respond agilely to market demands.

Chapter 7:
AI In Customer Experience

AI is reshaping the landscape of customer service, transforming traditional methods, and setting new standards for customer interactions. In this chapter, we'll explore how AI technologies, such as chatbots, virtual assistants, and machine learning algorithms, are being leveraged to enhance customer service experiences. By providing personalized, efficient, and proactive support, AI is empowering organizations to meet and exceed customer expectations. We will look at the various applications of AI in customer service, examining real-world examples and the benefits they bring. Moreover, we'll discuss the challenges and ethical considerations of integrating AI into customer service operations.

Enhancing Customer Service with AI Tools

Modern-day executives should be aware of how to utilize AI tools to enhance customer service that now provides personalized, efficient, and responsive customer interactions.

AI Chatbots and Virtual Assistants

AI chatbots and virtual assistants are revolutionizing customer service by providing instant, round-the-clock support, handling high volumes of inquiries with ease, and delivering personalized and efficient interactions that elevate the overall customer experience.

AI-powered chatbots and virtual assistants offer round-the-clock 24/7 customer support, ensuring that customer queries are addressed promptly at any time of the day. These tools can handle routine questions, provide information, and even guide customers through complex processes. By offering constant availability, organizations can enhance their reputation for reliability and customer-centricity.[cl] This continuous support minimizes customer frustration and elevates the overall customer experience, as customers can receive assistance whenever they need it without waiting for business hours. With the ability to instantly analyze and respond to customer inquiries, AI chatbots significantly reduce response times. This enhances the overall customer experience by providing quick and accurate solutions while also fostering greater customer satisfaction and loyalty.[cli] Quick responses not only resolve issues efficiently but also demonstrate to customers that their time is valued, thereby strengthening their trust in the brand.

During peak times, such as sales events or holidays, AI chatbots can manage high volumes of inquiries without delays. This ensures that customers do not face long waiting times, thereby contributing to higher satisfaction levels and more positive customer interactions.[clii] The scalability of AI chatbots allows organizations to maintain consistent service quality regardless of the number of inquiries, ensuring that all customers receive timely and effective support.

Below are a couple of AI chatbot platforms that your organization can use:

- Google's Dialogflow: Dialogflow is a powerful AI chatbot platform that allows organizations to create conversational interfaces for websites, apps, and messaging platforms. It uses natural language processing (NLP) to understand user queries and provide relevant responses. You can find more information on Dialogflow at dialogflow.cloud.google.com.

- Amazon Lex: It's an AI service for building conversational interfaces using voice and text. Amazon Lex provides advanced features like automatic speech recognition and natural language understanding to create engaging chatbots for customer service, virtual assistants, and more. You can find more information on Amazon Lex at aws.amazon.com/lex.

Sentiment Analysis and Customer Insights

Harnessing sentiment analysis and customer insights through AI empowers executives to understand and respond to customer emotions, anticipate needs, and deliver highly personalized and proactive support, thereby enhancing the overall customer service experience.

AI-driven sentiment analysis tools can assess customer emotions through their interactions, whether it's through text or voice. This helps executives to better understand the customer's feelings and respond appropriately by being able to tailor their support to address individual needs and concerns.[cliii] By detecting nuances in language and tone, sentiment analysis enables executives to gauge customer satisfaction levels and address potential issues proactively.

By analyzing past interactions and sentiment data, AI can identify customers who might need additional support or are likely to face issues. Proactive support can be provided to these customers, thereby enhancing their experience and preventing potential dissatisfaction by addressing problems before they escalate.[cliv] This proactive approach not only improves customer retention but also builds long-term loyalty by demonstrating a commitment to customer well-being and satisfaction.

Below are a couple of AI sentiment analysis and customer insights platforms that your organization can use:

- Google's Dialogflow: This platform uses natural language processing (NLP) to analyze text for emotional tone and adapt chatbot interactions accordingly. It can detect subtle emotional undertones in customer communications across various channels, such as emails and social media interactions. You can find more information on Dialogflow at dialogflow.cloud.google.com.
- Level AI: This platform offers automated scoring and real-time tracking of customer sentiment. It processes text, voice, and visual data to create a comprehensive emotional profile, allowing organizations to proactively address customer concerns and improve satisfaction. You can find more information on Level AI at thelevel.ai.

Multilingual Support

Implementing AI-powered multilingual support revolutionizes customer service by breaking language barriers to ensure effective communication and deliver consistent and high-quality service to a diverse global customer base.

AI-powered translation tools enable organizations to provide customer support in multiple languages so that language is not a barrier to excellent service. This is particularly important for global organizations with diverse customer bases as it allows them to effectively communicate and connect with customers around the world.[clv] By offering multilingual support, organizations can cater to a broader audience, enhancing their global presence and customer reach.

AI also ensures that customers receive a consistent level of service in any language, as it eliminates the variations that can come with human translation. This consistency helps maintain high standards of customer service.[clvi] Consistent quality across languages fosters a sense of reliability and professionalism while reinforcing the brand's reputation for excellence.

Below are a couple of AI multilingual support platforms that your organization can use:

- Avaamo: It's a conversational platform that supports over 114 languages and dialects. It automatically detects a customer's language and responds in their preferred language across all communication channels. This makes it ideal for organizations looking to provide seamless multilingual support globally. You can find more information on Avaamo at avaamo.ai.
- Helpshift: It offers real-time translation for over 150 languages. Helpshift features AI-powered chatbots and customizable workflows, making it easier for organizations to provide

accurate and efficient multilingual customer support. You can find more information on Helpshift at helpshift.com.

By embracing AI tools to enhance customer service, executives can achieve remarkable improvements in customer satisfaction and operational efficiency. AI-driven solutions provide valuable insights, streamline communication, and deliver personalized experiences that build stronger customer relationships. From chatbots that handle routine inquiries to advanced analytics that predict customer needs, AI can empower organizations to offer exceptional service while optimizing resources. Ultimately, integrating AI into your customer service strategies is not just a technical advancement but a commitment to delivering unparalleled value and fostering long-term loyalty.

Personalizing Marketing and Sales Strategies

In today's competitive marketplace, leveraging AI for personalizing marketing and sales strategies has become a game-changer for executives, enabling them to deliver tailored experiences that resonate deeply with their customers and ultimately drive significant growth.

Targeted Marketing Campaigns

Harnessing the power of AI for targeted marketing campaigns allows executives to precisely tailor their messages to individual customer segments.

AI can analyze customer data to create detailed segments based on behavior, preferences, and purchase history. This segmentation allows executives to tailor marketing campaigns to specific customer groups to increase the effectiveness of their efforts. By understanding the nuances of each segment, executives can make sure messages are crafted that resonate more deeply with their audience, leading to higher engagement and conversion rates. For example, AI can identify distinct customer segments such as "tech enthusiasts," "budget-conscious shoppers," or "luxury seekers," enabling marketers to design campaigns that speak directly to the unique interests and needs of each group.[clvii]

AI can predict customer behavior and preferences, thereby enabling executives to design marketing campaigns that resonate with their audience. Predictive analytics utilizes historical data and machine learning algorithms to forecast future trends and customer actions. For example, AI can analyze past purchase behavior to identify patterns and predict which products are likely to be of interest to a particular customer segment. Executives can then use this information to promote those products strategically, increasing the likelihood of purchase and improving overall campaign performance.[clviii]

Dynamic Pricing Strategies

Utilizing AI for dynamic pricing strategies enables executives to optimize their pricing models in real-time. It also ensures competitive advantage and maximizes profitability by continuously adapting to market trends, customer behavior, and competitor actions.

As AI algorithms can analyze market trends, competitor pricing, and customer demand in real-time to adjust prices dynamically, this dynamic pricing strategy ensures that organizations remain competitive while maximizing profits. By continuously monitoring external factors such as competitor price changes, supply and demand fluctuations, and seasonal trends, AI-driven pricing models can make real-time adjustments that optimize revenue and customer satisfaction.[clix]

AI can create personalized offers and discounts for individual customers based on their purchase history and preferences. This personalization not only incentivizes purchases but also builds customer loyalty. By leveraging data on individual customer behavior, such as past purchases, browsing history, and demographic information, AI can generate tailored promotions that resonate with each customer. For example, a loyal customer who frequently purchases athletic gear may receive exclusive discounts on new sports equipment, while a first-time visitor may be offered a special welcome discount.[clx]

Elevating Sales Processes

Elevating sales processes with AI empowers executives to streamline operations, enhance accuracy in forecasting, and prioritize high-potential leads.

AI can analyze sales data and market conditions to forecast future sales trends, thereby allowing executives to plan their inventory and sales strategies more effectively. By leveraging advanced algorithms and machine learning techniques, AI-driven sales forecasting models can provide accurate and timely predictions, enabling executives to make informed decisions about inventory management, production planning, and resource allocation. Accurate sales forecasting also helps executives identify potential risks and opportunities, ensuring they remain agile and responsive to market changes.[clxi]

AI can evaluate, and score leads based on their likelihood to convert, allowing sales teams to prioritize their efforts on high-potential prospects. This improves the efficiency and effectiveness of sales processes. By analyzing data points such as lead demographics, online behavior, and engagement history, AI-driven lead scoring models can assign a score to each lead, indicating their potential to convert into a paying customer. Sales teams can then focus their efforts on high-scoring leads, thus increasing the chances of successful conversions and maximizing the return on investment.[clxii]

Customer Journey Mapping

Leveraging AI for customer journey mapping allows executives to gain deep insights into customer interactions, optimize each touchpoint, and create seamless, personalized experiences.

AI can map out the entire customer journey, identifying key touchpoints and interactions that influence customer decisions. This helps executives to optimize each stage of the customer experience. By understanding the sequence of interactions that customers have with a brand, from initial awareness to post-purchase support, executives can identify critical touchpoints that impact customer satisfaction and loyalty. AI-driven customer journey mapping tools can provide valuable insights into customer behavior, allowing organizations to optimize touchpoints and deliver a seamless and personalized experience.[clxiii]

A couple of AI-powered customer journey mapping platforms are:

- MyMap.AI: This tool allows the visualization of detailed journey maps by inputting customer experience data. It offers AI-enabled chat interactions to create journey maps quickly and easily. You can find out more information on MyMap.AI at mymap.ai.

- Galaxy.AI: This platform helps map out customer journeys from awareness to advocacy with AI-powered insights. It offers comprehensive mapping, touchpoint analysis, and actionable insights. You can find out more information on Galaxy.AI at galaxy.ai.

By analyzing customer behavior, AI can predict future needs and preferences, allowing executives to proactively offer solutions and services that enhance the customer journey. By leveraging data on past interactions, purchase history, and contextual factors, AI can anticipate customer needs and provide timely and relevant recommendations. For example, an AI-driven system can analyze a customer's browsing history to identify products or services that they may be interested in, offering personalized suggestions that enhance the overall customer experience.[clxiv]

By integrating AI into marketing and sales strategies, executives can unlock new levels of personalization and efficiency that were previously unattainable. Dynamic pricing models ensure competitive and profitable pricing strategies while enhanced sales processes streamline operations and boost lead conversion rates. Additionally, AI-driven customer journey mapping allows for seamless, personalized experiences that build lasting customer loyalty. In essence, AI not only transforms marketing and sales efforts but also sets the stage for sustainable growth and success.

Exploring Real-time Price Adjustments in Greater Detail

As organizations strive to stay competitive in dynamic markets, the implementation of AI for real-time price adjustments has become a strategic advantage. AI-driven pricing models enable executives to respond swiftly to market changes, competitor actions, and customer demand fluctuations by continuously analyzing vast datasets. In this section, we examine the mechanisms and benefits of AI-powered real-time price adjustments, illustrating how executives can leverage these tools to optimize their pricing strategies, enhance profitability, and ensure the organization maintains a competitive edge.

- Market Trends Analysis: AI-powered tools can process vast amounts of data from various sources to identify emerging market trends. These tools analyze historical sales data, competitor pricing strategies, and consumer behavior patterns to predict future market movements. By understanding these trends, executives can adjust their pricing strategies proactively rather than reactively, ensuring they stay ahead of the competition.[clxv]

- Demand Forecasting: AI algorithms can accurately forecast demand by analyzing factors such as seasonality, promotional activities, and external economic conditions. By predicting periods of high or low demand, executives can optimize their pricing strategies to maximize revenue. For example, during peak demand periods, AI can suggest price increases to capture higher profits, while during low demand periods, it can recommend discounts to stimulate sales.[clxvi]

- Competitor Pricing Analysis: AI tools can continuously monitor competitor prices and provide real-time insights into pricing strategies. By understanding competitors' pricing tactics, executives can adjust their own prices to remain competitive while maximizing profitability. This dynamic pricing approach allows executives to respond quickly to market changes and maintain a competitive edge.[clxvii]

- Customer Demand Elasticity: AI can analyze customer data to determine the price elasticity of demand for different products. By understanding how sensitive customers are to price changes, executives can make informed decisions about price adjustments. For example, if a product has low price elasticity, executives can increase the price without significantly affecting sales volume, thereby increasing revenue. Conversely, for products with high price elasticity, executives can implement more competitive pricing strategies to attract price-sensitive customers.^{clxviii}

Exploring the intricacies of real-time price adjustments with AI reveals the profound impact these advanced tools can have on an organization's bottom line. By leveraging AI to continuously analyze market trends, competitor pricing, and customer demand, executives can make informed and dynamic pricing decisions that optimize revenue and customer satisfaction. AI's ability to predict demand fluctuations and assess price elasticity ensures that executives remain agile and competitive in a fast-paced market.

Examples of AI Creating Superior Customer Experiences

As AI continues to advance, its impact on customer experiences across various industries becomes increasingly profound. AI's ability to analyze vast amounts of data, predict customer behavior, and deliver personalized solutions is revolutionizing the way organizations interact with their customers. From enhancing shopping experiences in retail to providing tailored financial advice and optimizing healthcare services, AI-driven innovations are setting new standards for customer satisfaction and engagement. In this section, we explore a range of industry specific examples showcasing how AI is creating superior customer experiences by addressing unique needs and preferences with unparalleled precision and efficiency.

Retail Industry

In the retail industry, AI is transforming customer experiences by providing personalized shopping recommendations, streamlining virtual try-ons, and enhancing overall customer satisfaction through innovative and tailored solutions.

An online retail giant uses AI to analyze customer browsing and purchase history to provide personalized product recommendations. This approach has resulted in increased sales and customer satisfaction by ensuring that customers discover products that are relevant to their interests and needs. For example, if a customer frequently browses and purchases sportswear, the AI system will prioritize recommending related items, thereby enhancing the overall shopping experience. Moreover, AI can use collaborative filtering techniques to identify similar users and suggest products that have been well-received by others with similar tastes.[clxix]

Some fashion retailers have implemented AI-powered virtual try-on tools, allowing customers to see how clothes and accessories will look on them before making a purchase. These virtual try-ons use augmented reality and AI algorithms to create realistic simulations, thus enabling customers to make more informed decisions. By leveraging computer vision and deep learning techniques, these tools can accurately map the customer's body dimensions and create a virtual fitting room experience. This not only enhances the shopping experience but also significantly reduces return rates, as customers are more likely to be satisfied with their purchases.[clxx]

AI's transformative impact on the retail industry is setting new benchmarks for personalized shopping experiences, customer satisfaction, and overall organizational success.

Financial Services

In the financial services industry, AI is enhancing customer experiences by providing personalized financial advice, detecting and preventing fraud, and delivering tailored solutions that align with individual financial goals.

Banks and financial institutions use AI to provide personalized financial advice to their customers. By analyzing customer data, including spending habits, investment history, and financial goals, AI can recommend investment options, savings plans, and credit products that align with the customer's financial objectives. This personalized approach helps customers make informed financial decisions and helps to foster long-term loyalty. AI-driven financial advisors can also provide real-time insights and updates on market trends, ensuring that customers are always aware of the latest opportunities and risks.[clxxi]

AI algorithms can detect unusual patterns and behaviors in real-time and thus identify potential fraud attempts. By continuously analyzing transaction data, AI systems can flag suspicious activities, such as unusual spending patterns or transactions in atypical locations. This proactive approach ensures that customers' accounts and transactions are secure, building trust and confidence in the financial institution. Machine learning models can adapt and improve over time, becoming more effective at detecting and preventing fraud as they learn from new data.[clxxii]

AI's integration into financial services is revolutionizing the industry by delivering highly personalized, secure, and efficient solutions that meet the unique financial needs of each customer.

Hospitality Industry

In the hospitality industry, AI is enhancing guest experiences by providing personalized services, streamlining the check-in and check-out processes for guests, and offering tailored recommendations to make each stay unique and memorable.

Hotels and resorts leverage AI to provide personalized experiences for their guests. AI can analyze guest preferences and behavior to offer customized services, such as room settings, dining options, and activity recommendations. For example, if a guest frequently stays at a hotel chain and consistently requests a specific type of pillow, the AI system will ensure that this preference is noted and accommodated during future stays. Furthermore, AI can recommend activities and amenities based on a guest's past behavior, enhancing their overall experience. [clxxiii]

AI-powered systems streamline the check-in and check-out process, thereby reducing wait times and enhancing the overall guest experience. These systems can automatically assign rooms, process payments, and provide guests with digital room keys, allowing for a seamless and contactless experience. AI can also handle special requests and preferences to ensure that each guest's stay is tailored to their needs.[clxxiv]

AI's integration into the hospitality industry is redefining guest interactions by delivering highly personalized, efficient, and memorable experiences that elevate overall satisfaction and loyalty.

Healthcare Industry

In the healthcare industry, AI is transforming patient care by providing personalized health assistants, analyzing vast amounts of patient data for better treatment plans, and enhancing overall healthcare outcomes through innovative solutions.

AI health assistants can provide patients with personalized health advice, reminders for medication, and answers to common health queries. By leveraging natural language processing (NLP) and machine learning, these virtual assistants can offer accurate and timely information, ensuring that patients receive continuous support and care. For example, an AI health assistant can remind a patient to take their medication at specific times and provide information about potential side effects. These assistants can also monitor patient health metrics and provide early warnings for potential health issues.[clxxv]

AI can analyze patient data to provide doctors with insights and recommendations for treatment plans. By processing large datasets, including medical histories, lab results, and imaging studies, AI systems can identify patterns and correlations that may not be immediately apparent to human clinicians. This enhances the accuracy of diagnoses and the effectiveness of treatments, ultimately improving patient outcomes. AI can also assist in predicting patient outcomes and identifying potential complications, allowing for more proactive and preventive care.[clxxvi]

AI's transformative role in the healthcare industry is enhancing patient care, improving treatment accuracy, and delivering personalized, efficient healthcare solutions that significantly improve overall patient outcomes.

Travel and Tourism

In the travel and tourism industry, AI is also enhancing customer experiences by offering personalized travel recommendations, providing real-time assistance, and helping to streamline the entire travel process for a seamless journey for the customer.

Travel agencies and platforms use AI to offer personalized travel recommendations based on customer preferences and past travel history. By analyzing data such as previous destinations, preferred activities, and budget constraints, AI systems can suggest tailored travel itineraries that align with individual interests. This makes trip planning more convenient and ensures a more enjoyable travel experience. AI can also provide real-time updates and recommendations during the trip, thereby helping make the overall travel experience more enjoyable.[clxxvii]

AI chatbots assist travelers with booking changes, itinerary updates, and general inquiries, helping to ensure a seamless travel experience. These chatbots can provide real-time assistance, answer frequently asked questions, and handle routine tasks, allowing human agents to focus on more complex issues. Additionally, AI-powered chatbots can offer multilingual support, catering to a global customer base and enhancing accessibility.[clxxviii]

AI's integration into the travel and tourism industry is enhancing the travel experience for travelers by providing personalized, efficient, and seamless services that cater to each traveler's unique preferences and needs.

Telecommunications

In the telecommunications industry, AI is enhancing customer experiences by optimizing network performance, providing personalized service plans, and offering efficient customer support solutions tailored to individual needs.

AI helps telecom companies optimize their networks by predicting and addressing potential issues before they affect customers. By analyzing network performance data, AI systems can identify patterns that may indicate future problems, thus allowing executives to take proactive measures to ensure reliable service and customer satisfaction. AI can also optimize network traffic and allocate resources more efficiently, thus improving overall network performance.[clxxix]

By analyzing usage patterns, AI can recommend personalized service plans that best fit individual customer needs. For example, AI can identify customers who frequently exceed their data limits and suggest plans with higher data allowances or recommend cost-saving plans for customers who use minimal services. This enhances the customer experience by ensuring that each customer has a plan that aligns with their usage habits and preferences. AI can also predict future usage patterns and recommend plan adjustments proactively.[clxxx]

AI's implementation in the telecommunications industry is revolutionizing customer experiences by ensuring optimized network performance, personalized service plans, and efficient support. Moreover, it's ultimately driving higher customer satisfaction and loyalty.

By delving deeper into these examples, it becomes clear how AI is revolutionizing customer experiences across various industries.

Chapter 8:
Implementing AI In The
Organizational Structure

As executives strive to harness the power of AI to drive innovation and competitive advantage, implementing AI effectively within the organizational structure becomes a pivotal endeavor. This chapter provides a comprehensive guide to establishing a robust framework for AI integration, ensuring that the necessary infrastructure, resources, and governance are in place to support AI initiatives. We will explore strategies to cultivate a culture of innovation, encouraging collaboration, experimentation, and continuous learning among employees.

Moreover, we will address common challenges executives are encountering during the AI implementation process, such as data privacy concerns, technological limitations, and resistance to change. By providing practical insights and actionable steps, this chapter aims to equip executives with the knowledge and tools needed to successfully integrate AI into their organizational fabric.

Steps to Integrate AI into Organizational Strategy

The following are the steps executives must take to effectively integrate AI into their organizational strategy.

Assessing Current Capabilities and Needs

To start, conduct an AI readiness assessment to evaluate the current infrastructure and competencies within the organization. This assessment will help identify gaps and areas requiring improvement by examining aspects such as data availability, existing AI and machine learning capabilities, and the level of AI literacy among employees. For example, if the organization lacks sufficient data scientists or engineers, it might need to invest in hiring or training personnel.[clxxxi] Next, identify the specific business areas that could benefit from AI implementation, such as enhancing customer service through chatbots, optimizing supply chain logistics, or personalizing marketing campaigns. Setting clear goals and objectives for AI integration ensures alignment with the organization's overall strategy and the ability to measure success. For example, if the goal is to improve customer service, metrics such as customer satisfaction scores and response times can be used to gauge success.[clxxxii]

Developing a Strategic AI Roadmap

Create a strategic AI roadmap that outlines both short-term and long-term AI initiatives. Then, define clear milestones and timelines for these initiatives, making sure that resources, including budget and personnel, are adequately allocated. For example, the roadmap might include launching a pilot project for a customer service chatbot within six months, followed by scaling it up based on feedback and performance metrics. The roadmap should also include plans for ongoing monitoring and evaluation to be able to effectively adapt to changing needs and technologies.[clxxxiii]

Selecting the Right AI Technologies

Selecting the appropriate AI technologies is vital to successful implementation. Start by evaluating various AI tools and platforms based on the organization's specific needs. For example, if scalability is a key requirement, then consider cloud-based AI platforms that can easily handle increasing workloads. Next, assess the ease of integration of these technologies with existing systems and their support options, as this ensures that the chosen technologies align with the organization's AI goals. For example, if the goal is to improve customer insights, select AI tools that specialize in predictive analytics and customer data processing.[clxxxiv]

Building a Data Strategy

Develop a comprehensive data strategy to support AI initiatives. Establish data governance policies to ensure data quality and integrity by setting standards for data collection, storage, and usage. Create a robust data infrastructure capable of efficiently handling large volumes of data. For example, implementing scalable data storage solutions can facilitate seamless data management. Implement strong data privacy and security measures to protect sensitive information and comply with all relevant regulations, such as the General Data Protection Regulation (GDPR) and the California Consumer Privacy Act (CCPA). Be sure to work closely with the organization's legal department and IT department when implementing the necessary data privacy and security measures. A well-defined data strategy is essential for the success of AI projects, as high-quality data is the foundation of effective AI models. Have the organization's IT department regularly audit and clean data to remove inaccuracies and inconsistencies.[clxxxv]

Creating a Change Management Plan

Implementing AI involves significant organizational changes. To manage this transition smoothly, develop a change management plan. The key components of a change management plan typically include:

- Defining objectives and scope.
- Identifying the stakeholders.
- Developing a communication strategy.
- Outlining training and support measures.
- Managing any resistance.
- Establishing metrics for monitoring and evaluation.

The change management plan for implementing AI into an organization could look something like the following:

Change Management Plan for AI Implementation:

1. Objectives and Scope
- Objective: Successfully integrate AI technology to enhance decision-making, productivity, and operational efficiency.
- Scope: Implementation across key departments impacting approximately 200 employees.
2. Stakeholder Identification
- Executive Team: Sponsorship and oversight.
- IT Department: Technical integration and support.
- HR Department: Training and communication.
- Legal Department: Identify necessary data protection and privacy measures to be implemented.
- End-Users: Employees who will use the AI technology.
3. Communication Strategy

- Kick-off Meeting: Announce the AI initiative and outline the benefits.

- Regular Updates: Weekly updates by emails, updates in the newsletter, and posts on the organization's intranet to keep stakeholders informed.

- Feedback Mechanism: IT department sets up a dedicated email, aiconcerns@company.com, to be able to voice concerns and ask questions.

4. Training and Support

- Training Sessions: IT department to conduct mandatory training workshops for all end users.

- Documentation: IT department to provide clear and concise user manuals, FAQs, and helpful online resources.

- Support Team: A dedicated support team within the IT department to assist users during the transition.

5. Resistance Management

- Identify Potential Resistance: Engage with employees who might be resistant to the change.

- Address Concerns: Hold one-on-one meetings to address specific concerns and provide reassurance.

- Incentives: Offer incentives for early adoption and successful use of the AI technology.

6. Monitoring and Evaluation

- Metrics: Track AI usage, employee satisfaction, and productivity metrics by having the IT department implement AI-driven platforms to measure these.

- Review Meetings: Weekly reviews to monitor the progress and address any issues.

- Adjustments: Make the necessary adjustments based on the feedback and the performance data received.

Implementation Timeline:

- Week 1: Announce the change and hold the kick-off meeting.
- Weeks 2-4: Conduct training sessions and provide documentation.
- Weeks 5-8: Monitor implementation, provide support, and gather feedback and performance data.
- Week 9+: Review the progress and make necessary adjustments.

Once the change management plan has been created, employee engagement is critical. First, communicate the benefits of AI to all employees (and stakeholders) to build support and enthusiasm, highlighting how AI can enhance efficiency, reduce costs, and create new opportunities. Then, provide training and education to enhance AI literacy within the organization, ensuring that employees understand how AI will impact their roles and how to utilize AI tools effectively. For example, offering workshops or online courses on AI fundamentals can help bridge knowledge gaps. Finally, address resistance by involving employees in the AI implementation process and addressing their concerns transparently. This could include conducting surveys to gather feedback and incorporating their suggestions into the implementation plan.[clxxxvi]

Implementing AI Solutions

It's smart and prudent to start with pilot AI projects to test their feasibility and gather valuable insights. These pilot projects can identify potential challenges and refine AI models before full-scale implementation. For example, a pilot project could involve implementing an AI-powered recommendation system for a small segment of the customer base to gauge its effectiveness and make necessary adjustments. Once pilot projects are successful, then scale them to larger deployments. Be sure to continuously monitor and evaluate the AI model's performance to ensure alignment with the organization's goals and to be able to make the necessary adjustments. For example, setting up dashboards to track KPIs can provide real-time insights into AI system performance. Regularly update AI systems with new data and algorithms to maintain their effectiveness and the organization's competitive edge. This might involve retraining machine learning models with fresh data to improve accuracy and relevance.[clxxxvii]

Although digital transformations are critical for organizations to remain competitive, 70% of attempted digital transformations fail. The primary reasons digital transformations fail in organizations are the following:

- Lack of strategy with clear goals.
- Insufficient leadership commitment.
- Limited employee engagement and the absence of a change strategy.
- Poor monitoring of progress.
- Failure to scale beyond initial pilots.

Thus, it's necessary to be cognizant of all of these reasons why digital transformations, such as AI implementation, fail so you can overcome these hurdles towards AI transformation within your organization.[clxxxviii]

Building an AI Team and Fostering a Culture of Innovation

Creating an AI team and nurturing a culture of innovation helps to harness the full potential of AI technologies, drive creativity, and stay ahead in today's competitive landscape.

Assembling a Cross-Functional AI Team

Building a diverse and cross-functional AI team leverages various perspectives and expertise. The team should include data scientists, AI engineers, domain experts, and project managers. Data scientists are responsible for analyzing and interpreting complex data and applying statistical and machine-learning techniques to extract meaningful insights. AI engineers design, build, and deploy AI models and systems, ensuring their scalability and reliability. Domain experts provide industry-specific knowledge, guiding AI development to align with the organization's needs. Project managers oversee project timelines, resources, and deliverables, ensuring that AI projects are completed on time and within budget. It's essential to encourage collaboration and full cooperation between these roles to be able to effectively leverage the collective knowledge and experience by setting clearly defined roles and responsibilities for each team member, which ensures accountability and effective execution of AI projects. Regular team meetings and open communication channels help align the team's efforts and promptly address any challenges.[clxxxix]

Developing AI Skills and Expertise

Invest in training programs and workshops to help develop the necessary AI competencies within the organization. Also, encourage employees to independently pursue AI certifications and advanced degrees to deepen their knowledge and skills. Be sure to provide employees with access to online courses and the ability to attend industry conferences, as well as offer hands-on experience with AI technologies to help foster a culture of continuous learning and professional development. The organization should offer to reimburse any costs associated with these additional learning initiatives. Employees should also be encouraged to participate in AI communities, forums, and meetups to stay updated on the latest AI advancements, trends, and best practices. By fostering a culture of continuous learning, executives can ensure that their employees are equipped with the necessary skills to navigate the rapidly evolving AI landscape.[cxc]

Encouraging Experimentation and Innovation

Creating an environment that encourages experimentation and innovation helps to drive AI advancements. Provide resources and support for employees to explore new AI ideas and projects, as this helps to foster a culture of creativity and continuous improvement. Innovation labs or incubators can serve as dedicated spaces where employees can develop and test AI solutions in a controlled setting. These labs should be equipped with the necessary tools and technologies to support experimentation. Recognizing and rewarding innovative efforts helps to motivate employees and reinforces the importance of creativity in the organizational culture. Celebrate successes and encourage employees to learn from failures, as this can create an environment where they feel encouraged to take risks and experiment with new ideas.[cxci]

Promoting Collaboration and Knowledge Sharing

Facilitate regular meetings and workshops to share AI knowledge and best practices across the organization to help foster collaboration and knowledge sharing. Be sure to encourage collaboration with external partners, such as universities and research institutions, as this helps the organization stay at the forefront of AI research and development. Utilize collaboration tools, such as project management software, communication platforms, and knowledge repositories, to enhance communication and teamwork and help ensure that the AI projects benefit from collective insights and expertise. These tools also help to track progress and share updates. Ultimately, establishing a culture of open communication and knowledge sharing can lead to more innovative solutions and better problem-solving capabilities.[cxcii]

Recognizing and Rewarding Innovation

Implementing recognition programs to reward employees for their contributions to AI initiatives helps motivate and retain top talent. Be sure to celebrate successful AI projects and share achievements with the entire organization to build enthusiasm and support for future endeavors. It also helps to provide incentives, such as bonuses, promotions, and public recognition, for employees who engage in AI projects, as it reinforces the importance of innovation in the organizational culture. It's also important to create a fair and transparent recognition system. Recognizing and rewarding efforts not only motivates employees but also encourages them to continue exploring new ideas and solutions.[cxciii]

Overcoming Common Challenges and Obstacles

Overcoming common AI challenges and obstacles unlocks its full potential, ensuring its ethical use and fostering trust and collaboration between the AI systems and their human users. The following are some of the common AI challenges and obstacles executives must be ready to overcome when implementing AI in the organization.

Managing Data Quality and Availability:

High-quality data is essential for effective AI implementation. Implementing robust data collection and preprocessing techniques ensures that the data used is accurate and relevant. Data preprocessing involves cleaning and transforming raw data into a format suitable for analysis. Address data silos (isolated collections of data within an organization that are inaccessible to other departments, leading to inefficiencies and hindered decision-making) by integrating data from different sources into a unified system to enable a comprehensive analysis. Develop strategies to handle missing or incomplete data to ensure that AI models have the information they need to perform accurately. Furthermore, data governance policies should be established to ensure the long-term maintenance and integrity of data quality.[cxciv]

Addressing Ethical and Bias Concerns:

Ethical considerations should be paramount in AI development and deployment. Implementing ethical guidelines ensures that AI systems operate fairly and transparently. Bias in AI can result from unrepresentative training data, algorithmic biases, or unintended consequences of AI deployment. Regularly audit AI systems for biases and take corrective actions as needed to help maintain fairness and accountability. Foster a culture of ethical AI practices by training employees on the importance of fairness, transparency, and accountability in AI decision-making to build trust and credibility. Executives should establish ethical review boards to oversee AI projects and ensure compliance with the ethical standards they have set.[cxcv]

Ensuring Regulatory Compliance:

Stay informed about any relevant regulations and compliance requirements related to AI by working closely with the organization's legal department to avoid legal issues and maintain public trust. Make sure the organization's legal department implements measures to ensure that its AI systems adhere to legal standards, such as data protection laws and industry-specific regulations. The legal department should also develop a compliance framework to monitor and enforce regulatory adherence to ensure that the organization's AI initiatives remain compliant and trustworthy. Executives should appoint compliance officers or committees to oversee AI projects and to further ensure adherence to regulatory requirements and help mitigate risks. Ultimately, regularly reviewing and updating AI compliance policies is essential to keep up with changing regulations and industry standards.[cxcvi]

Managing Organizational Change and Resistance:

Organizational change can be challenging, and resistance to AI implementation tends to be common. Clearly communicate the benefits of AI to all levels of the organization and emphasize how it will enhance operations and create new opportunities to help gain support. Engage employees in the AI implementation process to also help build buy-in and support. Be sure to address any concerns proactively and provide support to employees as they adapt to new AI technologies to help pave the way for a smooth transition. Thus, change management strategies, such as involving employees in decision-making, providing training and resources, and maintaining open communication, can help overcome resistance and facilitate successful AI adoption.[cxcvii]

Scaling AI Solutions:

Planning for scalability is essential to ensure that AI solutions can grow within the organization. Consider scalability from the outset and choose technologies and infrastructures that can accommodate growth. Be sure to monitor the AI system's performance and make necessary adjustments to help maintain its scalability. Invest in scalable infrastructure and technologies, such as cloud computing and distributed systems. Executives should establish processes to regularly review and optimize AI models to help make sure they continue to perform well as they scale.[cxcviii]

Maintaining Security and Privacy:

Security and privacy are critical concerns in AI implementation. Ensure that the organization's IT department structures robust security measures to protect AI systems and data from cyber threats and safeguard sensitive information. NIST, or the National Institute of Standards and Technology, emphasizes the importance of continuously improving and expanding shared evaluation frameworks to address evolving threats. They recommend adaptive evaluations, proactive simulated attacks and efforts to uncover new vulnerabilities even as systems improve. Moreover, NIST recommends that task-specific attack performance should be analyzed alongside aggregate performance to gain a comprehensive understanding of risks. Testing the success of attacks over multiple attempts is advised by NIST to produce more realistic and robust evaluation results.[cxcix]

Also, make sure that the organization's legal department complies with all applicable data privacy regulations to maintain the integrity of the organization and the trust of its stakeholders, employees and customers. The IT department must regularly update its security protocols to address emerging threats and vulnerabilities to protect and maintain the reliability of AI systems. Executives should conduct regular security assessments and audits to identify and address potential vulnerabilities. It's critical that executives establish a culture of security awareness and train employees on best practices for data protection to further enhance the security of AI systems.[cc]

Ultimately, implementing AI systems within an organization requires careful planning, a robust framework, and a culture of innovation. By addressing common challenges and fostering a collaborative environment, executives can effectively integrate AI into their operations and harness its full potential to drive innovation and competitive advantage.

Chapter 9:
AI Ethical and Legal Considerations

Navigating the realm of AI demands an unwavering commitment to ethical and legal principles, ensuring that the technology's advancement aligns with societal values and protects the rights of individuals. This chapter analyzes the key ethical and legal considerations that must guide the development and deployment of AI systems. We will explore paramount issues such as data privacy, algorithmic bias, transparency, and accountability and examine how these factors influence the responsible use of AI.

Additionally, we will discuss the importance of adhering to regulatory frameworks and industry standards to safeguard the interests of all stakeholders. By addressing these ethical and legal dimensions, executives will better understand the principles that should underpin the development of AI technologies, fostering a balanced approach that prioritizes both innovation and societal well-being.

Addressing Ethical Dilemmas in AI Usage

Confronting ethical dilemmas in AI usage requires a thoughtful balance between technological innovation and moral responsibility.

Fairness and Bias

AI systems can be prone to biases present in their training data, which can result in unfair treatment of individuals and groups. It's crucial to identify and mitigate these biases to ensure fairness. Bias detection techniques include statistical analysis of training data to identify imbalances, use fairness-aware algorithms, and continuously monitor AI outputs for discriminatory patterns. For example, analyzing the dataset used to train an AI hiring tool might reveal that certain demographics are underrepresented. Implement algorithms designed to account for these imbalances to help ensure fair and unbiased treatment. Perform regular audits and updates to AI models to address new biases that may emerge. Also, include diverse stakeholders in the development process to help identify and address biases that may not be immediately apparent. This collaborative approach ensures that a variety of perspectives are considered, thereby leading to more equitable AI systems. Additionally, employing techniques such as adversarial testing, where AI systems are deliberately exposed to challenging scenarios, can help uncover hidden biases. Incorporating feedback loops allows for continuous improvement and adaptation of AI models to address fairness concerns effectively.[cci]

Mitigating bias in AI systems is an ongoing challenge. Regular training and awareness programs for AI developers can also contribute to reducing biases. Beyond statistical analysis and fairness-aware algorithms, another technique is fair representation learning, which aims to learn unbiased data representations. Moreover, using synthetic data can help balance training datasets without compromising privacy. An example of fairness in practice is IBM's AI Fairness 360 toolkit, which provides metrics and algorithms to help detect and mitigate bias in AI models.[ccii]

Privacy and Data Protection

AI applications often rely on large volumes of personal data, making privacy and data protection paramount. Safeguarding personal information involves having your IT department implement data anonymization and encryption techniques to protect against unauthorized access. Data anonymization is the process of transforming personal data in such a way that it can no longer be traced back to individual entities, ensuring privacy and compliance with data protection regulations. It makes sure that even if the data is accessed without authorization, individuals cannot be identified. Encryption adds another layer of protection by ensuring that the data cannot be read without the appropriate decryption key. Balancing the need for data access with privacy rights requires transparent data practices and obtaining informed consent from data subjects.[cciii]

Organizations, with the guidance of their legal departments, must comply with all relevant data protection regulations, such as the GDPR, to avoid legal repercussions. Non-compliance with GDPR, for example, can lead to hefty fines and damage to the organization's reputation. Additionally, having the organization's IT department implement privacy-enhancing technologies (PETs), such as differential privacy and federated learning, can further protect personal data while enabling the ability to derive valuable insights. Differential privacy is a mathematical technique used to ensure individual privacy by adding controlled noise to data, allowing for statistical analysis without having to reveal personal information. Federated learning is a decentralized machine learning approach that trains models collaboratively across multiple devices or servers while keeping the data localized, thus ensuring privacy. PETs are tools and techniques designed to protect personal data by minimizing its exposure, enhancing user privacy, and ensuring compliance with data protection regulations. Transparent data practices and robust security measures are essential for protecting individual privacy while still leveraging the benefits of AI. For example, informing individuals about what data is being collected and how it will be used is essential for maintaining trust. [cciv]

PETs are continually evolving. For example, homomorphic encryption allows computations on encrypted data without decrypting it, ensuring data privacy throughout the process. Another innovative approach is secure multi-party computation, where multiple parties can jointly compute a function over their inputs while keeping those inputs private. Companies like Apple use differential privacy to collect aggregate data without compromising individual user privacy. Emphasizing data minimization and adopting privacy-by-design principles can further strengthen data protection. [ccv]

Executives must make sure that strong encryption protocols are implemented, as they are essential for securing data both at rest and in transit. Encryption transforms readable data into an unreadable format, making it accessible only to those with the decryption key. This ensures that even if data is intercepted or accessed by unauthorized parties, it remains protected. Executives should make sure that advanced encryption standards (AES) are used and regularly update encryption keys to mitigate risks. [ccvi]

Executives should make sure that anonymization is implemented as additional security. Anonymization is a vital process that ensures privacy by removing personally identifiable information (PII) from datasets, making individuals unidentifiable. This technique is crucial for protecting privacy while still allowing executives to analyze data for insights. Methods such as data masking (obscuring or anonymizing sensitive information), tokenization (converting sensitive data into non-sensitive equivalents called tokens), and differential privacy can be employed to anonymize data effectively. Additionally, executives should make sure that re-identification risk assessments are performed to ensure anonymized data cannot be traced back to individuals.[ccvii]

Executives should make sure that granular access controls are implemented as they ensure that only authorized personnel have access to sensitive data. Role-based access control (RBAC) and attribute-based access control (ABAC) are commonly used to enforce access policies based on users' roles and attributes. RBAC is a method of regulating access to computer systems and data based on the roles assigned to individual users within an organization. ABAC is an authorization model that determines access rights based on attributes associated with users, resources, actions, and the environment. Regular audits and monitoring of access logs are essential to detect and respond to unauthorized access attempts promptly.[ccviii]

To ensure the integrity and security of the digital ecosystem, executives must remain vigilant and committed to upholding rigorous data protection standards.

Transparency and Explainability

Transparency and explainability are essential for building trust in AI systems. Make sure AI systems are transparent by documenting decision-making processes and making them accessible to stakeholders. For example, an AI system used in healthcare to recommend treatments should provide an explanation of the factors influencing its decisions. Develop methods for making AI decisions more understandable by using explainable AI (XAI) (aims to provide transparent and interpretable AI models that can offer clear explanations for their decisions and actions) techniques, such as providing feature importance scores and decision trees. Feature importance scores quantify the contribution of each input feature in a model to its overall predictive power, helping to identify which features are most influential in making predictions. Decision trees are graphical representations used in machine learning and data analysis that split data into branches based on feature values (e.g., customer age, customer income, etc.), leading to a decision or prediction at each leaf node. These techniques help users understand the reasoning behind AI decisions, fostering trust and accountability.[ccix]

Transparent AI practices are particularly important in sensitive applications like finance and healthcare, where understanding the decision-making process is crucial. For example, in finance, an AI system used for credit scoring should explain why a particular score was assigned, allowing users to understand and contest the decision if necessary. Furthermore, adopting standardized documentation practices, such as model cards and datasheets for datasets, can enhance transparency by providing detailed information about the AI model and its training data. Model cards are detailed documentation tools that provide essential information about machine learning, including their performance, limitations, and intended use cases. Dataset nutrition labels are standardized documentation tools that provide essential information about a dataset's contents, quality, and potential biases, helping users assess its suitability for specific use cases. Continuous user education and engagement further support transparency efforts, ensuring that stakeholders have the proper knowledge and tools to understand AI decisions. [ccx]

Enhancing transparency and explainability requires both technical and organizational efforts. Techniques such as LIME (Local Interpretable Model-agnostic Explanations) and SHAP (SHapley Additive exPlanations) help interpret complex models by attributing importance to individual features. LIME is a technique designed to provide understandable and human-interpretable explanations of complex, black-box machine learning models at the individual prediction level. SHAP is a method used in machine learning to fairly distribute the contribution of each feature to the overall prediction, providing interpretable insights into the model's decisions.

Moreover, interactive visualizations can provide intuitive explanations of AI decisions. Interactive visualizations are graphical representations of data that enable users to engage with and explore the information through dynamic elements such as filters, zoom, and clickable features. Organizations like Google have adopted model cards and dataset nutrition labels to document and communicate the details of their AI models.[ccxi]

Ensuring transparency in AI systems involves providing clear and concise explanations in plain English on how AI algorithms process data and make decisions. This includes documenting the data sources, model architectures, and decision-making processes used in AI applications. Ultimately, transparency helps build trust with users and stakeholders and facilitates compliance with regulatory requirements.[ccxii]

Accountability and Liability

Defining accountability structures within organizations for AI systems is critical to being able to address AI errors and malfunctions. Establishing responsibility within an organization for AI-driven outcomes involves assigning roles and responsibilities to the individuals or teams overseeing AI systems. For example, if an AI system used in AVs malfunctions and causes an accident, it should be clear who within the organization is responsible for the AI's performance so measures internally can be taken to ensure that best practices are changed and lessons are learned going forward. Proactive risk assessment and mitigation strategies, such as scenario analysis and contingency planning, can further enhance accountability by preparing organizations to handle potential AI failures effectively. [ccxiii]

To establish accountability, create clear governance structures, and define roles and responsibilities within the organization as to AI systems. Executives should implement AI ethics committees or responsible AI boards that can establish and implement AI standards and as well as oversee AI projects and ensure ethical considerations are addressed. For example, Microsoft has established a Responsible AI Standard that outlines best practices for developing and deploying AI responsibly. Moreover, develop internal incident response plans for AI failures. Organizations implementing AI systems should also work with legislatures to craft responsible and ethical AI legislation in the jurisdictions they conduct business.[ccxiv] Regular audits, impact assessments, and accountability reports can help organizations demonstrate their commitment to ethical AI practices and compliance with data protection regulations.[ccxv]

As to legal liability, normal tort and contract laws would apply if there is damage or harm caused by an AI failure. Tort law, which deals with civil wrongs and negligence, can be used to address harms caused by AI systems, as the individuals that are harmed would have a civil claim in tort against the organization that owns the AI system. Contract law can also come into play, especially when there are contractual agreements between parties regarding the use and performance of AI systems. Note that the application of these laws to AI, however, can be complex and may vary depending on the jurisdiction and specific circumstances surrounding the case. As with the development of anything new, case law will begin to develop and set a precedent in the area of AI law as these complex issues are sorted out by the courts. Moreover, states and countries will continue to pass statutes and regulations to address AI accountability and liability issues.[ccxvi] Once again, it's imperative that an organization's legal department stay up to date on all the applicable AI laws that could affect an organization and educate the organization's executives on the best practices to be implemented as a result thereof.

Ethical AI Frameworks

Various ethical frameworks to help guide AI development and use. Integrating ethical considerations into AI design and deployment involves adhering to principles such as fairness, transparency, accountability, and human-centricity. Executives can refer to established guidelines, such as the IEEE Global Initiative on Ethics of Autonomous and Intelligent Systems, when developing their own AI ethical standards.

Case studies on ethical AI implementations also provide valuable insights into best practices and lessons learned. For example, a case study on the ethical deployment of AI in healthcare might highlight how transparency in AI decision-making processes helped build trust among patients and healthcare providers. These frameworks provide a structured approach for incorporating ethical considerations into AI development, ensuring that AI systems are designed and deployed in a manner that respects human rights and promotes social good.[ccxvii]

Obtaining informed consent from individuals whose data is used for AI training is one of the most critical ethical considerations. Organizations must provide clear and accessible information about how data will be used, the purpose of data processing, and any potential risks involved. Consent mechanisms should be designed to allow individuals to make informed decisions and easily withdraw consent if so desired.[ccxviii]

Executives should establish an ethics review board and conduct regular ethics audits to help an organization adhere to ethical standards and address any new ethical dilemmas. Adhering to ethical AI frameworks involves continuous evaluation and necessary revisions. Also incorporate ethics impact assessments at different stages of AI development to help identify and address any ethical concerns early on.[ccxix]

Collaborate with academic institutions and civil society organizations to help provide diverse perspectives and enhance ethical practices. Case studies, such as the use of AI in disaster response by the International Federation of Red Cross and Red Crescent Societies (IFRC), highlight how ethical AI can make a positive impact. Regular ethics training for AI teams and fostering an organizational culture that prioritizes ethics are also essential.[ccxx]

By fostering a culture of ethical awareness and responsibility, executives can ensure that their AI systems contribute positively to society.

Human-Centric AI

AI systems should be designed to enhance human well-being and promote social good. Human-centric AI practices ensure that the benefits of AI are distributed equitably, promoting social good and enhancing human well-being. Ensuring that AI respects human rights and autonomy involves prioritizing user needs and minimizing harm. For example, AI systems in education should support teachers and students, enhancing the learning experience without infringing on privacy or fairness. Human-centric AI should also be inclusive, providing equitable access to its benefits across different demographics and geographies. Promote inclusive AI practices by including diverse perspectives in AI development and address potential disparities in AI impact. This can involve consulting with communities that are often underrepresented in technology development to ensure their needs and perspectives are considered in the development and implementation of AI technologies.[ccxxi]

Moreover, AI systems designed with user feedback loops and participatory design processes can ensure that AI solutions are tailored to meet the diverse needs of users, fostering a more inclusive and beneficial impact. Design human-centric AI with a focus on user experience and social impact. Employ participatory design methodologies, where users are involved in the design process, to ensure that AI systems meet their needs and preferences. Examples of human-centric AI include AI-powered education tools, such as Khan Academy's personalized learning platform, which adapts to individual student needs. Promote digital literacy by providing resources to help users understand and engage with AI to further enhance its positive impact.[ccxxii]

Ethical Audits and Impact Assessments

Conducting ethical audits evaluates AI systems' compliance with ethical standards and identifies areas for improvement. Ethical audits involve reviewing AI development processes, decision-making criteria, and potential impacts on stakeholders. By implementing impact assessments helps executives understand the societal implications of AI deployment, ensuring that AI systems contribute positively to society. Tools and methodologies for ethical auditing and impact assessment provide structured approaches to evaluate AI systems' ethical performance. These processes should be embedded into the AI development lifecycle to ensure continuous ethical compliance.[ccxxiii]

Addressing ethical dilemmas in AI usage requires a commitment to transparency, accountability, and fairness to ensure that these technologies are developed and applied in a way that benefits society as a whole.

Understanding the Legal Landscape and Compliance Issues

Navigating the intricate legal landscape and compliance issues surrounding AI is absolutely essential for organizations, their executives, and their legal departments, as it involves understanding a complex web of laws and potential risks that impact the development, deployment, and ongoing utilization of AI technologies.

Regulatory Frameworks

AI governance is shaped by various global and regional regulations and standards. Key regulatory bodies, such as the European Commission and the National Institute of Standards and Technology (NIST), play significant roles in AI oversight. A comparative analysis of AI regulatory approaches in different countries helps executives understand the diverse legal requirements and adapt their practices accordingly. Staying updated with the evolving regulatory landscape is crucial for an organization's legal department to ensure compliance and avoid potential legal pitfalls. Executives must monitor legislative developments, participate in industry forums, and collaborate with legal experts to interpret and implement regulatory requirements effectively.[ccxxiv]

Data Protection and Privacy Laws

Understanding and complying with data protection and privacy laws, such as the California Consumer Privacy Act (CCPA) and the General Data Protection Regulation (GDPR), is essential for organizations using AI applications. Once again, an organization's legal department must stay abreast of all of the applicable data protection laws in the jurisdictions where the organization conducts or intends to conduct business.

Some of the compliance requirements include obtaining consent for data collection, implementing data protection measures, and providing individuals with rights to access, rectify, and delete their data. Non-compliance with data protection laws can lead to severe legal and financial consequences, emphasizing the need for robust data governance practices. Executives must invest in data protection technologies, conduct regular data audits, and educate employees on data privacy best practices.[ccxxv]

Below is a summary of just a few of the major privacy and data protection laws that executives should be aware of, but as always, it's absolutely critical that an organization's legal department, along with its IT department, be extremely familiar with all of the pertinent privacy and data protection laws. Numerous class action lawsuits have been filed in recent years against organizations alleging that they have not properly protected their customers' data, have not provided the proper disclosures, and/or did not obtain the proper consent from their customers.

The California Consumer Privacy Act (CCPA), enacted in 2020, grants California resident's specific rights regarding their personal data, including the right to know what data is being collected, the right to delete their data, and the right to opt out of the sale of their data. Organizations must provide transparent privacy policies, implement mechanisms for consumers to exercise their rights, and ensure compliance with data protection obligations to avoid legal repercussions.[ccxxvi]

The General Data Protection Regulation (GDPR), enacted in the European Union, sets stringent requirements for data protection and privacy. Organizations that process the data of EU residents must comply with GDPR provisions, including obtaining explicit consent for data processing, providing individuals with the right to access and erase their data, and ensuring data portability. GDPR also mandates that organizations conduct Data Protection Impact Assessments (DPIAs) for high-risk data processing activities to identify and mitigate potential privacy risks.[ccxxvii]

The Personal Data Protection Act (PDPA), passed in 2014, governs the collection, use, and disclosure of personal data in Singapore. It requires organizations to obtain consent for data processing, provide individuals with access to their data, and ensure data accuracy and protection. The act also establishes the Personal Data Protection Commission (PDPC) to enforce compliance.[ccxxviii]

The Personal Information Protection and Electronic Documents Act (PIPEDA), enacted in 2000, applies to private sector organizations that collect, use, or disclose personal information in the course of commercial activities. Although PIPEDA primarily applies to private sector organizations that collect, use, or disclose personal information in the course of commercial activities within Canada, it can also apply to organizations outside of Canada if they handle personal information about Canadian residents in the context of commercial activities. It requires organizations to obtain consent, limit data collection to what is necessary, and protect data with appropriate security measures. Individuals have the right to access and correct their personal information.[ccxxix]

The Brazilian General Data Protection Law (LDPD), effective from August 2020, regulates the processing of personal data in Brazil. It mandates obtaining explicit consent for data processing, providing individuals with rights to access, correct, and delete their data, and ensuring data protection by design. The National Data Protection Authority (ANPD) oversees enforcement and compliance.[ccxxx]

The Data Protection Act 2018 (DPA 2018) is the United Kingdom's implementation of the GDPR with additional provisions specific to the United Kingdom. It sets out requirements for data protection, including obtaining consent, providing data subjects with rights to access and erase their data, and conducting Data Protection Impact Assessments (DPIAs) for high-risk activities. The Information Commissioner's Office (ICO) is the regulatory authority that oversees enforcement and compliance.[ccxxxi]

The Health Insurance Portability and Accountability Act (HIPAA), enacted in 1996, establishes standards for the protection of health information in the United States. It requires healthcare providers, insurers, and their business associates to implement safeguards to protect patient data, obtain patient consent for data sharing, and provide patients with the right to access their health information.[ccxxxii]

Again, these laws represent just a few of the major data protection and privacy regulations currently in effect around the world. As AI and data-driven technologies continue to evolve, the regulatory frameworks are expected to become more comprehensive and stringent. Future regulations may require organizations to demonstrate ethical data handling practices, obtain informed consent from individuals for AI training purposes, and ensure transparency and accountability in AI systems. Compliance with these regulations will absolutely necessitate ongoing efforts by legal departments to stay informed about legal developments and then have the IT departments adapt robust data protection strategies accordingly.

Intellectual Property and AI

Intellectual property (IP) considerations are crucial in AI development, including patenting AI inventions and addressing copyright issues related to AI-generated content. Navigating IP challenges involves understanding the legal frameworks governing AI innovations and protecting proprietary technologies. Collaborative AI projects and open-source AI initiatives require clear agreements on IP ownership and usage rights to prevent disputes. It's also important for an organization's legal departments to stay abreast of emerging IP issues, such as the ownership of AI-generated works and the patentability of AI algorithms.[ccxxxiii]

The ownership of copyright for AI-generated content varies depending on jurisdiction. Here is a summary of the ownership of copyright for AI-generated content in the United States and the European Union:

- United States: In the United States, copyright requires human authorship for ownership. This means that AI-generated works are not eligible for copyright protection and are considered to be in the public domain. The U.S. Copyright Office issued guidance explaining, however, that "a work containing AI-generated material will also contain sufficient human authorship to support a copyright claim" where the author made a creative arrangement of the AI-generated work or substantially modified it.[ccxxxiv]

- European Union: The EU has not yet established a clear stance on AI-generated content. However, the European Commission is working on regulations that may address this issue in the future.[ccxxxv]

- Other Jurisdictions: Different countries have varying approaches to AI-generated content. For example, some countries may allow for limited copyright protection if there is significant human involvement in the creation process.[ccxxxvi]

Liability and Risk Management

Risk assessment and mitigation strategies involve identifying potential legal risks, developing contingency plans, and securing appropriate insurance coverage. [ccxxxvii] Legal liabilities associated with AI use and deployment must be carefully managed by an organization's legal department. These liabilities can be multifaceted and can vary depending on the jurisdiction and the specific application of the AI technology. Here are some key considerations:

- Product Liability: Organizations may be held liable for damages caused by their AI systems, especially if the AI is integrated into products and services that consumers interact with. This includes potential personal injury, property damage, and/or financial losses.[ccxxxviii]

- Accountability and Transparency: AI systems' autonomy and ability to learn can make their decision-making processes opaque and difficult to trace. This complexity increases the risk of harm and makes it challenging to pinpoint the exact cause of harm and hold any party accountable.[ccxxxix]

- Laws and Regulations: Governments and legal bodies worldwide are working to update their laws and regulations to address AI liability. For example, the European Union's GDPR and the proposed Artificial Intelligence Act aim to hold developers and users accountable for the outcomes of AI systems.[ccxl]

- Contract Law and Insurance: In the absence of specific AI laws, contract law plays a crucial role in determining liability. Contracts between developers, manufacturers, and users often include clauses defining responsibilities in the event of AI failure. AI liability insurance policies are also becoming more prevalent, providing coverage for damages caused by AI system failures.[ccxli]

- Risk Assessments: Conducting AI impact and risk assessments is essential for identifying potential risks associated with AI technology. These assessments help executives make informed decisions about using AI and proactively address ethical, legal, and operational challenges. Executives should work closely with the organization's legal department and its insurance broker to assess the potential risks and formulate the best strategy to protect the organization through insurance coverage and best practices.[ccxlii]

Case studies of legal disputes in AI contexts also offer valuable lessons for organizations' legal departments to navigate complex liability issues.[ccxliii]

Suggested Best Practices for AI Data Privacy and Security

Below is a summary of the essential current best practice measures to protect an organization's sensitive information and ensure adherence to data protection regulations when integrating and working with AI platforms. Again, make sure you work with your organization's legal department to create its best practices before implementing them, and be sure to continue to review them with legal counsel on a regular basis.

- Data Minimization: Adopt the principle of data minimization by collecting only the data necessary for specific AI purposes. Limiting data collection reduces the risk of exposure and ensures compliance with privacy regulations. Executives must make sure that regular reviews of data collection practices are conducted to identify and eliminate unnecessary data processing.[ccxliv]

- Secure Data Storage: Implement secure AI data storage solutions, such as encrypted databases, PETs, and secure cloud services, to protect sensitive information. Regularly update and patch storage systems to address vulnerabilities and prevent data breaches. Additionally, executives must make sure that data backup and disaster recovery plans are implemented to ensure data availability and integrity in case of incidents.[ccxlv]

- Data Classification Protocols: Identify and classify AI data based on its sensitivity and importance to the organization. Restrict access to sensitive data based on classification levels. Again, encrypt data and use PETs to protect it from unauthorized access.[ccxlvi]

- Synthetic AI Data: Consider utilizing Synthetic data as it eliminates the use of real personal information, thereby reducing privacy risks and ensuring compliance with regulations like GDPR. Moreover, generating synthetic data is often cheaper than collecting and maintaining real-world datasets and is generally easily scalable and can be safely shared with all team members as well as collaborative partners without any privacy concerns.[ccxlvii]

- Data Lifecycle Management: Establish clear policies for how long AI data should be retained and when it should be deleted. Conduct regular audits to ensure data is being managed according to lifecycle policies. Implement archiving solutions for long-term storage of data that is no longer actively used but must be retained for compliance.[ccxlviii]

- Data Ownership and Accountability: Clearly define who owns the AI data and who is responsible for its management. Establish an accountability framework that outlines the roles and responsibilities for data management.[ccxlix]

- Employee Training and Awareness: Educate employees about the AI data privacy and security best practices through regular training programs and awareness campaigns. Employees should be aware of their roles and responsibilities in safeguarding data and understanding the importance of compliance with data protection laws. Training should cover topics such as recognizing phishing attempts, handling sensitive data securely, and immediately reporting security incidents. Formalize the AI data privacy policy and security best practices in a formal organizational policy that employees can easily access and review whenever needed.[ccl]

- Incident Response and Management: Develop and implement an incident response plan so that your organization can promptly address AI data breaches and security incidents. The plan should outline procedures and metrics for detecting, as well as the procedures for containing and mitigating incidents, including notifying affected individuals and the necessary regulatory authorities as required by law. Conduct regular drills and simulations to ensure the effectiveness of the incident response plan and improve preparedness.[ccli]

- Continuous Review and Improvement: Executives, along with the legal department, should continuously review its best practices on a regular basis and make any necessary changes when appropriate.

By implementing these robust data privacy and security measures, an organization can protect its sensitive information, maintain public trust, and comply with evolving regulatory requirements.

Thus, addressing the ethical and legal considerations of AI is paramount to ensuring its responsible development and deployment by organizations and their executives. By fostering transparency, accountability, and fairness in AI systems, executives can mitigate risks such as data privacy breaches, algorithmic bias, and unintended consequences. Executives must adhere to regulatory frameworks and industry standards to safeguard the interests of all stakeholders and build public trust in AI technologies.

Chapter 10:
The Future Of Work With AI

As we stand on the cusp of a new technological era, the future of work is being profoundly reshaped by the incredible resurgence of AI. AI's rapid evolution is transforming traditional job roles, creating new opportunities, and redefining the skills required to thrive in the modern workforce. This chapter delves into the multifaceted impact of AI on the world of work, exploring how executives and employees can adapt to these changes, harness the potential of AI-driven technologies, and navigate the challenges and ethical considerations that arise.

The Impact of AI on the Workforce

As AI technologies become more sophisticated, they are driving significant changes in job roles, skill requirements, and organizational structures. Automation, machine learning, and data analytics are transforming traditional industries, creating new opportunities for innovation and efficiency. However, this technological shift also brings challenges, such as job displacement and the need for workforce reskilling. This section explores the multifaceted impact of AI on the workforce by examining how executives can adapt to these changes, leverage AI's potential, and address the ethical considerations that arise in this evolving landscape.

Job Displacement and Creation

AI will significantly impact the workforce by automating routine tasks, thereby leading to job displacement in some areas while simultaneously creating new roles and opportunities in AI development, oversight, and related fields.

The impact of AI on the job market is a topic of much debate and analysis. According to the World Economic Forum (WEF), AI and other information processing technologies are expected to displace around 92 million jobs by 2030. However, it's also anticipated that AI will create approximately 170 million new jobs during the same period. Goldman Sachs offers a more sobering estimate, predicting that up to 300 million jobs could be lost or degraded due to AI by 2030. This includes jobs that may be significantly altered or diminished in quality due to automation and AI advancements.[cclii]

AI will automate a wide array of routine and repetitive tasks, which will lead to the displacement of certain jobs. For example, administrative tasks such as data entry, scheduling, and basic customer service interactions can be performed more efficiently by AI-driven systems. Manufacturing processes like assembly line work and quality inspections can also be automated, thus reducing the need for manual labor. However, this shift will create new job opportunities in AI development, maintenance, and oversight. Professionals with expertise in AI programming, machine learning, data analysis, and AI system management will be in high demand. As AI technology advances, it will drive the creation of roles focused on developing, implementing, and managing AI systems.[ccliii]

As AI takes over certain tasks, new roles will emerge that require human oversight, creativity, and problem-solving skills. For example, roles in AI ethics, data science, AI training, and AI system auditing will become more prominent. These positions will focus on ensuring that AI systems are fair, transparent, and aligned with ethical standards. Additionally, the need for data scientists to analyze and interpret the vast amounts of data generated by AI systems will grow significantly. New job categories, such as AI ethicists, who ensure compliance with ethical guidelines, and AI trainers, who design and refine AI algorithms, will become essential.[ccliv]

While AI may displace some jobs by automating routine tasks, it will also create new opportunities that will drive the evolution of the workforce.

Changes in Job Functions

As AI becomes increasingly integrated into the workplace, it's reshaping job functions by augmenting human capabilities and shifting the skills required for success in various roles.

AI will augment human capabilities, thus allowing employees to focus on more complex and strategic tasks. This augmentation can lead to increased job satisfaction and productivity as routine and monotonous tasks are offloaded to AI systems. For example, AI-powered tools can assist with data analysis, market research, and decision-making processes, allowing employees to concentrate on strategic planning and creative problem-solving. In healthcare, AI can support doctors by analyzing medical images, allowing them to focus on patient care and treatment.[cclv]

As AI tools become more integrated into the workplace, the demand for skills in AI literacy, data analysis, and digital competency will increase. Employees will need to adapt to new technologies and acquire skills related to AI implementation, management, and oversight. This shift will necessitate ongoing education and training programs to ensure the workforce remains competitive. Executives must invest in upskilling their employees to equip them with the necessary knowledge and skills to work alongside AI systems.[cclvi]

Ultimately, AI integration will transform job functions by enhancing human capabilities and necessitating new skills.

Impact on Different Industries

AI is transforming various industries by enhancing efficiency, improving decision-making, and driving innovation across sectors such as manufacturing, healthcare, retail, and financial services.

- Manufacturing: AI will revolutionize manufacturing through predictive maintenance, quality control, and automation of production lines. AI systems can predict equipment failures before they occur, reducing downtime and maintenance costs. By analyzing data from sensors and machines, AI can identify patterns that indicate potential issues and trigger maintenance activities proactively. Additionally, AI-driven quality control systems ensure that products meet high standards by detecting defects with greater accuracy and consistency than manual inspections. Automated production lines powered by AI can operate 24/7, increasing productivity and efficiency.[cclvii]

- Healthcare: In healthcare, AI will enhance diagnostics, treatment planning, and patient care through advanced data analysis and predictive analytics. AI algorithms can analyze medical images, electronic health records, and genetic data to identify patterns and correlations that may not be apparent to human clinicians.

This leads to improved diagnostic accuracy and the development of personalized treatment plans. AI-powered systems can also assist in drug discovery by analyzing vast datasets to identify potential drug candidates and predict their efficacy.[cclviii]

- Retail: Retail businesses will use AI for inventory management, personalized customer experiences, and demand forecasting. AI can analyze customer behavior, preferences, and purchasing patterns to provide personalized recommendations and targeted marketing. This enhances the overall shopping experience and increases customer loyalty. AI-driven inventory management systems can optimize stock levels, ensuring that products are available when and where customers need them, reducing overstock and stockouts. Demand forecasting powered by AI helps retailers anticipate customer demand and plan their inventory accordingly.[cclix]

- Financial Services: AI will impact financial services by improving fraud detection, automating customer service, and enhancing investment strategies. AI systems can analyze transaction data in real-time to detect fraudulent activities while reducing the risk of financial losses. AI-powered chatbots can provide efficient and personalized customer service, handling routine inquiries and transactions. In investment management, AI algorithms can analyze market data, identify trends, and optimize investment portfolios to maximize returns.[cclx]

Overall, AI is revolutionizing industries by driving efficiency, enhancing decision-making, and fostering continuous innovation.

Skills Needed for the AI-Driven Economy

In the rapidly evolving AI-driven economy, a diverse set of skills is required to thrive and stay competitive. Technical skills, such as AI and machine learning, data analysis, and programming, form the foundation of working with intelligent systems. However, soft skills like critical thinking, problem-solving, adaptability, flexibility, and emotional intelligence are equally essential to enable executives to navigate complex challenges and collaborate effectively.

Hybrid skills that combine technical expertise with domain-specific knowledge, digital literacy, and ethical awareness are also crucial for leveraging AI tools responsibly and efficiently. This comprehensive skill set will empower executives to harness the full potential of AI, allowing them to innovate and excel in their respective fields.

Technical Skills

Technical skills are essential for leveraging AI effectively, encompassing expertise in AI and machine learning, data analysis, and programming.

- AI and Machine Learning: Understanding the basics of AI and machine learning is crucial for executives in the AI-driven economy. This includes knowledge of supervised and unsupervised learning, neural networks, deep learning techniques, and reinforcement learning. Mastery of these concepts enables executives to develop, deploy, and optimize intelligent systems. For example, understanding how neural networks work and how to fine-tune them is essential for building accurate predictive models. Moreover, familiarity with specialized areas such as computer vision, natural language processing (NLP), and reinforcement learning expands a professional's capability to tackle diverse AI projects.[cclxi]

- Data Analysis and Interpretation: The ability to analyze and interpret data is a key skill in the AI-driven economy. This involves understanding statistical methods, data visualization techniques, and data mining processes. Effective data analysis allows executives to derive actionable insights and drive organizational decisions. For example, being able to use statistical techniques to identify trends and patterns in data can help executives make informed decisions about product development and marketing strategies. Proficiency in advanced analytical methods such as regression analysis, clustering, and time-series analysis is particularly valuable.[cclxii]

- Programming and Software Development: Proficiency in programming languages such as Python, R, and Java, as well as experience with AI frameworks and tools like TensorFlow, PyTorch, and scikit-learn, are essential. Programming skills enable executives to build and implement AI models, automate tasks, and integrate AI solutions into existing systems. For example, being able to write efficient code to preprocess data, train machine learning models, and deploy them in production environments is valuable and extremely helpful. Furthermore, knowledge of version control systems like Git, software development practices, and cloud computing platforms enhances a professional's ability to work on collaborative AI projects.[cclxiii]

Mastering technical skills in AI, data analysis, and programming is now a fundamental component every executive should embrace to be able to leverage AI effectively for the organization.

Soft Skills

Soft skills, such as critical thinking, problem-solving, adaptability, and emotional intelligence, are critical for thriving in an AI-driven economy.

- Critical Thinking and Problem-Solving: The ability to think critically and solve complex problems is invaluable in an AI-driven economy. This involves analyzing situations, identifying underlying issues, and developing creative solutions. Critical thinking enables executives to navigate challenges that AI systems may not be able to handle. For example, when AI models produce unexpected results, critical thinking skills are necessary to diagnose the issue and implement corrective measures. Moreover, the ability to evaluate the ethical implications of AI decisions and make informed judgments is crucial.[cclxiv]

- Adaptability and Flexibility: Being adaptable and flexible in a rapidly changing technological landscape is an essential skill. This means being open to new ideas, technologies, and methodologies and being willing to learn and adapt continuously. Adaptability ensures that executives can keep pace with technological advancements and remain relevant in their fields. For example, as new AI tools and techniques emerge, professionals must be willing to update their skills and incorporate these innovations into their workflows. The ability to transition between different projects, roles, and industries seamlessly is also valuable.[cclxv]

- Emotional Intelligence: The ability to understand and manage emotions, both in oneself and in others, is critical for navigating the changing dynamics of the workplace. Emotional intelligence enables executives to build strong relationships, communicate effectively, and manage stress. For example, being able to empathize with colleagues and clients and manage conflicts constructively is essential for maintaining a positive and productive work environment. Moreover, fostering a culture of collaboration and inclusivity is essential in AI-driven organizations.[cclxvi]

Thus, developing soft skills as an executive is essential to thrive in an AI-driven economy.

Hybrid Skills

Hybrid skills combine technical expertise with domain-specific knowledge, digital literacy, and ethical awareness to leverage AI effectively.

- Tech-Savviness: Combining technical skills with domain-specific knowledge to effectively utilize AI tools is essential. This involves understanding the specific needs and challenges of an industry and applying AI solutions to address them. Tech-savviness allows executives to bridge the gap between the technical and functional aspects of AI. For example, a professional in the healthcare industry must understand both medical principles and AI technology to develop effective diagnostic tools. Similarly, in finance, combining knowledge of financial markets with AI expertise can lead to better investment strategies.[cclxvii]

- Digital Literacy: Understanding and leveraging digital tools and platforms to enhance productivity and collaboration is vital. This includes proficiency in using cloud services, collaborative software, and digital communication tools. Digital literacy ensures that executives can effectively navigate and utilize digital resources. For example, being skilled in using collaboration platforms can enhance teamwork and project management, leading to more efficient workflows. Additionally, understanding cybersecurity principles and data protection practices is crucial in handling sensitive information.[cclxviii]

- Ethical Awareness: Recognizing and addressing ethical considerations related to AI, such as bias, privacy, and transparency, is paramount. This involves understanding the ethical implications of AI technologies and ensuring that they are developed and used responsibly. Ethical awareness promotes trust and accountability in AI systems. For example, executives must be able to identify and mitigate biases in AI models to ensure fair and equitable outcomes. Moreover, addressing concerns related to data privacy and security is essential to maintain public trust.[cclxix]

Hybrid skills, which combine technical expertise with domain-specific knowledge, digital literacy, and ethical awareness, are essential for leveraging AI effectively and responsibly as an executive.

Thriving as an executive in the AI-driven economy requires a well-rounded skill set that encompasses technical expertise, soft skills, and hybrid capabilities. Mastery of AI and machine learning, data analysis, and programming forms the technical backbone for working with intelligent systems. Complementing these with critical thinking, problem-solving, adaptability, and emotional intelligence provides executives with the necessary skills to navigate complex challenges and collaborate effectively. Furthermore, combining technical skills with domain-specific knowledge, digital literacy, and ethical awareness ensures responsible and efficient use of AI tools.

Upskilling and Reskilling Programs

As the integration of AI reshapes the workforce, upskilling and reskilling employees become paramount to ensure they are equipped with the necessary skills to thrive in an AI-driven economy. Continuous learning and practical, hands-on training provide employees with the knowledge and experience required to work effectively with AI tools and technologies. By fostering a culture of lifelong learning and offering diverse educational opportunities, executives can empower their workforce to adapt to rapid technological advancements, thereby enhancing their competence and confidence in leveraging AI for organizational success.

- Continuous Learning Opportunities: Providing employees with access to continuous learning opportunities is essential for keeping the workforce updated with the latest AI advancements. This can be achieved through a variety of educational resources, such as online courses, workshops, webinars, and certification programs in AI, machine learning, data science, and related fields. Organizations can partner with online education platforms like Coursera, edX, and Udacity to offer tailored learning paths that align with employees' roles and career aspirations. Continuous learning not only enhances technical skills but also fosters a culture of lifelong learning. Moreover, offering incentives such as tuition reimbursement, professional development allowances, and recognition programs can motivate employees to engage in continuous learning.[cclxx]

- On-the-Job Training: Implementing on-the-job training programs allows employees to gain practical experience with AI

178

tools and technologies in their work environment. This hands-on approach enables employees to apply theoretical knowledge to real-world scenarios, thus enhancing their understanding and competence. On-the-job training can include job rotations, mentorship programs, collaborative projects, and shadowing opportunities that expose employees to different aspects of AI implementation. For example, a manufacturing company might rotate employees through various AI-driven processes to provide them with a comprehensive understanding of AI applications in production, quality control, and maintenance.[cclxxi]

By investing in upskilling and reskilling programs, executives can ensure their employees remain agile, knowledgeable, and capable of leveraging AI technologies.

Collaboration Between Industry and Education

Collaboration between industry and education is also vital for preparing a workforce that is well-equipped to navigate the AI-driven economy. By forging strong partnerships, organizations, and educational institutions can create curricula that align with industry needs, ensuring that graduates possess the skills and knowledge required to excel in AI-related fields. These collaborations can also provide students with valuable hands-on experience through internships, research projects, and mentorship opportunities.

Collaborating with educational institutions to develop curricula that align with industry needs is crucial for preparing students for AI-driven careers. These partnerships can involve co-creating courses, offering internships, supporting research initiatives, and providing guest lectures from industry professionals. Educational institutions can benefit from industry insights, while organizations gain access to a talent pool equipped with relevant skills. For example, a tech company might work with a university to develop a specialized AI program that includes real-world projects, internships, and mentorship opportunities.[cclxxii]

Developing industry-specific training programs that focus on the unique needs and challenges of different sectors is essential. These programs can address the distinct applications of AI in industries such as healthcare, finance, manufacturing, and retail. For example, training programs for the healthcare sector can focus on AI in diagnostics, personalized medicine, and healthcare management. In contrast, programs for the financial sector might emphasize AI in fraud detection, risk assessment, and algorithmic trading. By tailoring training programs to specific industries, executives can ensure that employees acquire the skills and knowledge necessary to excel in their respective fields.[cclxxiii]

Effective collaboration between industry and education bridges the skills gap and ensures a well-prepared workforce for the AI-driven economy.

Promoting a Culture of Innovation

Promoting a culture of innovation is crucial for organizations aiming to stay competitive in the AI-driven economy.

Executives should encourage employees to experiment with AI tools and technologies and to think creatively about their applications. Providing the necessary resources, time, and support for experimentation creates an environment where employees feel safe to take risks and explore new ideas. This can lead to breakthrough innovations and continuous improvement. For example, an organization might establish an innovation lab where employees can collaborate on AI projects, test new technologies, and develop prototypes. Moreover, implementing hackathons, innovation challenges, and idea-sharing platforms can inspire employees to think outside the box and contribute innovative solutions.[cclxxiv]

Supporting intrapreneurial initiatives allows employees to develop and implement AI-driven projects within the organization. Intrapreneurial refers to the entrepreneurial mindset and activities undertaken by employees within an established organization. Intrapreneurship fosters a sense of ownership and motivation as employees work on projects that align with their interests and expertise. Executives can create intrapreneurship programs, provide funding, and recognize successful projects to encourage participation. For example, an organization might offer employees the opportunity to pitch AI-related projects and provide funding, resources, and mentorship to bring those projects to fruition. Recognizing and rewarding intrapreneurial efforts through awards, promotions, and public acknowledgment can further incentivize employees to innovate.[cclxxv]

An innovative culture drives continuous improvement and enables executives to capitalize on the full potential of AI technologies.

Addressing Ethical and Social Implications

Addressing the ethical and social implications of AI is important as the technology becomes increasingly integrated into various aspects of society. Ensuring responsible AI deployment involves recognizing and mitigating biases, safeguarding data privacy, and promoting transparency in AI decision-making processes.

Providing training on the ethical implications of AI, including issues related to bias, privacy, and transparency, is essential for responsible AI deployment. Ethics training can help employees recognize and mitigate biases in AI models, ensure data privacy, and promote transparency in AI decision-making processes. This training can be integrated into regular professional development programs and supplemented with workshops, seminars, and case studies that illustrate ethical dilemmas and best practices. For example, employees might participate in workshops that explore real-world scenarios where AI systems exhibited bias and discuss strategies for mitigating such biases.[cclxxvi]

Engaging with stakeholders, including employees, customers, and regulators, is vital for addressing concerns and ensuring responsible AI deployment. Executives can hold forums, workshops, and consultations to gather feedback, discuss potential impacts, and develop strategies for ethical AI implementation. Stakeholder engagement fosters trust and collaboration by creating a shared understanding of AI's benefits and risks. For example, an organization might organize a town hall meeting to discuss the implications of a new AI-driven product, solicit feedback from customers and employees, and address any concerns. Moreover, engaging with regulators and industry groups can help ensure compliance with ethical guidelines and foster industry-wide standards for responsible AI use.[cclxxvii]

Addressing ethical and social implications is essential for fostering public trust and ensuring responsible AI deployment in organizations.

By embracing continuous learning, fostering collaboration between industry and education, promoting a culture of innovation, and addressing ethical and social implications, executives can navigate the complexities of the AI-driven economy with confidence. The convergence of human ingenuity and AI technology holds the potential to drive unprecedented advancements, creating a more efficient, inclusive, and dynamic workforce.

Chapter 11:
Measuring AI Success

In an era where AI plays an increasingly pivotal role in transforming industries and driving innovation, measuring the success of AI implementations is critical for executives striving to achieve their strategic objectives. Effective measurement goes beyond mere technical performance, and it encompasses evaluating the impact of AI on organizational processes, customer experiences, and overall organizational efficiency. By establishing clear metrics, aligning AI initiatives with organizational goals, and continuously monitoring outcomes, executives can gain valuable insights into the effectiveness of their AI deployments. This chapter explores the key methodologies and best practices for measuring AI success along with specific AI platforms that measure these key indicators, ensuring that executives can maximize the value of their AI investments and drive sustainable growth.

Key Performance Indicators for AI Initiatives

To effectively measure the success of AI initiatives, executives must establish key performance indicators (KPIs) that align with their strategic objectives and capture the impact of AI on various aspects of their operations. KPIs serve as essential metrics that help executives assess the performance, efficiency, and effectiveness of their AI implementations. By defining clear and relevant KPIs, executives can monitor progress, identify areas for improvement, and ensure that AI initiatives deliver tangible value.[cclxxviii]

Operational Efficiency

Operational efficiency is a critical measure of an organization's ability to effectively utilize its resources and streamline processes. By integrating AI technologies, executives can achieve unprecedented levels of efficiency and productivity. AI-driven automation, time-saving strategies, and cost-saving measures can significantly reduce manual effort, optimize operations, and lower expenses.[cclxxix] This section will explore the KPIs related to measuring operational efficiency.

Process Automation Rates

Process automation rates measure the extent to which AI technologies have successfully automated tasks and processes within an organization, highlighting the efficiency and productivity gains achieved through reduced manual effort. Automation can streamline repetitive tasks such as data entry, customer service responses, and inventory management, significantly reducing the need for manual labor and human intervention. Higher automation rates often lead to improved efficiency and productivity.[cclxxx]

A couple of AI-enabled automation platforms that measure process automation rates are:

- Inkyma's platform provides metrics to measure the effectiveness of AI and automation, including ROI, process efficiency, cost savings, accuracy improvements, customer satisfaction, and employee productivity. You can find more information on Inkyma at inkyma.com.

- Google Cloud offers KPIs for measuring the success of generative AI, focusing on model accuracy, operational efficiency, user engagement, and financial impact. You can find more information on Google Cloud at google.com.

A couple of AI-driven automation tools are:

- Blue Prism is known for its intelligent automation solutions. Blue Prism enables organizations to automate complex business processes across various departments (human resources, finance and accounting, customer service, sales and marketing, supply chain and logistics, IT and support), thus improving efficiency and reducing operational costs. You can find more information about Blue Prism at blueprism.com.

- Automation Anywhere's AI platform offers a comprehensive suite of automation tools, including RPA and intelligent automation, to streamline workflows and enhance productivity. Specifically, it can: (1) Invoice Processing, automate the extraction, validation, and processing of invoices to reduce manual effort and minimize errors; (2) Customer Onboarding, streamlining the onboarding process for new customers by automating data entry, verification, and account setup tasks; (3) Payroll Processing, automating payroll calculations, tax deductions, and direct deposits to ensure timely and accurate payments to employees; (4) Order Management, managing and processing customer orders efficiently by automating order entry, inventory checks, and shipment tracking; and (5) Data Migration, facilitating the transfer of data between systems with minimal disruption, ensuring data integrity and consistency. You can find more information about Automation Anywhere at automationanywhere.com.

Time Saved

Quantifying time saved involves measuring the reduction in hours required to complete specific tasks or processes due to the implementation of AI technologies, enabling executives to allocate their resources more efficiently and focus on higher-value activities. This can include reductions in the time spent on administrative tasks, report generation, and decision-making processes. AI can analyze vast amounts of data at high speeds, providing insights and recommendations much faster than humans can. For example, AI-powered chatbots handle customer inquiries instantly, freeing up human agents for more complex issues.[cclxxxi]

A couple of AI-powered tools that automate time management as well as measure the reduction in hours required to complete specific tasks or processes due to the implementation are:

- RescueTime automates team time management. It offers features like automatic time tracking, project tracking, and timesheet generation. This AI-powered tool helps users track their time and provides insights into how they spend their day. It identifies time-wasting activities and offers organizations personalized recommendations to improve their productivity. While primarily a time management tool, it can track productivity and provide insights into how much time is saved by automating certain tasks. You can find more information on RescueTime at rescuetime.com.
- Toggl Track's time-tracking software uses AI to analyze work patterns and provide reports on time saved through automation and efficiency improvements. You can find more information on Toggle Track at toggl.com.

- Timely is an AI-driven time-tracking tool that automates team time management, making it easier to monitor and optimize work hours and ensuring efficient use of time. You can find more information on Timely at timely.com.

Cost Savings

Cost savings measure the financial impact of AI implementation, encompassing reductions in labor costs, optimized resource usage, and decreased operational expenses, ultimately enhancing an organization's financial efficiency and overall profitability. Predictive maintenance powered by AI can foresee equipment failures, allowing for timely repairs and reducing downtime. This not only saves costs associated with unexpected breakdowns but also extends the lifespan of equipment.[cclxxxii]

A few AI-driven platforms that are able to measure the cost savings and financial impact on your organization from AI implementation are:

- Wally is an AI-driven tool that offers insights into your organization's spending habits, helping you to identify areas where you can cut costs and save money. You can find more information on Wally at mywally.ai.
- Cleo uses a chatbot interface, Cleo makes budgeting for your organization more engaging and helps users manage their

finances more effectively, leading to potential cost savings. You can find more information on Cleo at meetcleo.com.

- Alteryx is a data analytics platform that includes tools for building and deploying AI models. It also provides features for measuring the ROI of AI implementations and tracking cost savings. You can find more information about Alteryx at alteryx.com.

- Microsoft Azure AI offers a suite of AI services and tools that can build, deploy, and manage AI models. It includes capabilities for measuring the performance and cost savings of AI implementations. You can find more information about Microsoft Azure AI at azure.microsoft.com.

A couple of AI predictive maintenance platforms that foresee maintenance failures are:

- C3.ai offers an AI-based predictive maintenance platform called C3 AI Reliability, which enables organizations to predict and prevent asset failures by providing comprehensive monitoring across critical and non-critical assets. The platform identifies anomalous behaviors, provides prioritized alerts, recommends prescriptive actions, and enables collaboration through an integrated workflow. You can find out more information on C3.ai at c3.ai.

- IBM Maximo is an enterprise-grade solution that leverages AI and IoT technologies for advanced predictive analytics. It focuses on AI-driven insights to predict and prevent failures, offering features like AI-based anomaly detection, asset monitoring, lifecycle management, and predictive alerts. You can find more information on IBM Maximo at ibm.com/products/maximo.

Through the strategic implementation of AI initiatives, executives can achieve remarkable advancements in operational efficiency, driving sustained growth and a lasting competitive advantage.

Accuracy and Quality

Accuracy and quality are fundamental metrics that determine the success and reliability of AI implementations. Ensuring high levels of accuracy in AI models and maintaining quality standards in products or services is crucial for organizations to build trust and achieve desired outcomes. By minimizing errors, improving prediction accuracy, and enhancing overall quality, AI technologies can significantly contribute to the consistency and excellence of organizational operations.[cclxxxiii] This section will explore the KPIs related to measuring accuracy and quality, highlighting the transformative impact of AI on delivering precise, high-quality outcomes.

Error Reduction

Error reduction measures the decrease in errors or defects resulting from AI implementation, ensuring higher accuracy and reliability in organizational processes and outcomes. AI systems can perform tasks with high precision and consistency, thereby reducing the likelihood of human errors. This is crucial in industries like healthcare, manufacturing, and finance, where errors can be costly or dangerous. For example, AI algorithms can detect anomalies in medical imaging more accurately than human radiologists.[cclxxxiv]

Here is an AI-driven application that can measure the decrease in errors or defects resulting from AI implementation:

- Fraime by Saiwa's platform offers AI-powered tools for anomaly detection in manufacturing. By identifying deviations early in the production process, it helps measure and reduce defects, providing insights into the effectiveness of AI implementation. You can find out more information about Fraime by Saiwa at saiwa.ai.

Here are a couple of AI-enable platforms that are able to detect errors in real-time and provide detailed analytics on the reduction of errors and defects:

- Core BTS Quality Control is an AI-driven quality control system that uses machine learning and computer vision to detect defects in real-time. It provides detailed analytics on the reduction of errors and defects, allowing organizations to measure the impact of AI on their operations. You can find out more information on Core BTS Quality Control at corebts.com.

- Testim is an advanced test automation platform that uses machine learning to streamline software testing. It can run automated tests for web applications and improves test creation and maintenance by automatically adapting to changes in the application, ensuring high test reliability and faster delivery of quality software. One of Testim's standout features is its use of AI to maintain tests as over time, applications change and evolve, and maintaining tests can become time-consuming and error-prone. Testim's AI can identify changes in the application's user interface (UI) and automatically update the tests to reflect these changes, reducing the need for manual intervention and ensuring that the tests remain accurate and up-to-date. You can find more information on Testim at testim.io.

Prediction Accuracy

Prediction accuracy evaluates how well AI models make predictions or classifications, using metrics such as accuracy, precision, recall, and F1 score to gauge performance and ensure reliable and insightful outcomes for various applications. Accurate predictions are vital for applications like demand forecasting, fraud detection, and personalized marketing.[cclxxxv]

A couple of AI-powered applications that are able to evaluate how well AI models make predictions or classifications are:

- Weights & Biases platform provides tools for tracking, visualizing, and analyzing machine learning experiments. It helps evaluate model performance by offering detailed metrics, visualizations, and comparisons while enabling users to understand how well their AI models are making predictions. You can find out more information on Weights & Biases at wandb.ai.

- MLflow is an open-source platform for managing the end-to-end machine learning lifecycle. MLflow includes tools for tracking experiments, packaging code into reproducible runs, and sharing and deploying models. It provides comprehensive metrics and evaluation reports to assess the accuracy and effectiveness of AI models. You can find out more information on MLflow at mlflow.org.

A couple of AI-driven platforms that perform predictions are:

- SAS Predictive Analytics provides advanced analytics solutions that help organizations predict future trends and behaviors. Their platform uses AI and machine learning to analyze historical data, identify patterns, and make accurate predictions, which can be applied to areas such as customer behavior, risk management, and supply chain optimization. You can find more information on SAS Predictive Analytics at sas.com/en_us/home.html.

- Amazon Forecast is another great example of an AI platform for prediction accuracy is Amazon Forecast. It's a fully managed service that uses machine learning to deliver highly accurate forecasts and is particularly useful for time series data, such as sales, demand, and inventory levels. You can find more information about Amazon Forecast at aws.amazon.com.

Quality Improvements

Quality improvements assess how AI technologies enhance the quality of products or services, leading to higher standards and better customer satisfaction by effectively identifying and addressing defects or issues in real-time. AI-driven quality control systems can identify defects in products more effectively than human inspectors, leading to higher quality standards. For example, AI algorithms can analyze production line images to detect defects in real time, ensuring that only products meeting the highest standards are shipped to customers.[cclxxxvi]

- Automated Visual Inspection Systems: These systems use AI-powered cameras and image recognition algorithms to inspect products for defects or inconsistencies. They can detect minute imperfections that might be missed by human inspectors, ensuring higher quality standards.[cclxxxvii]

o   Kitov.ai is a platform that offers AI-based visual inspection planning and inspection for various industries, including electronics, automotive, and medical devices. Their platform uses AI and 3D computer vision to find cosmetic and mechanical defects, reducing inspection errors and improving overall product quality. You can find more information about Kitov.ai at kitov.ai.

o   Averroes.ai is also known for its high accuracy because this software also provides automated AI visual inspection and virtual metrology solutions across multiple industries. Their system integrates seamlessly with existing inspection equipment and provides real-time monitoring and analysis of defects, thereby enhancing quality control and reducing manual intervention. You can find more information about Averroes.ai at averroes.ai.

- Predictive Maintenance: AI algorithms can analyze data from machinery and equipment to predict potential failures before they occur. By scheduling maintenance activities proactively, executives can prevent unexpected breakdowns and maintain consistent product quality.[cclxxxviii]

o   C3.ai is an AI-based platform that helps organizations predict and prevent asset failures, offering comprehensive monitoring and proactive maintenance. You can find more information for C3.ai at c3.ai.

o Dingo Trakka is another AI-based platform that specializes in asset health management. It combines data analytics and machine learning to optimize asset performance in heavy industries, such as mining and oil and gas. You can find more information about Dingo Trakka at dingo.com/solutions/trakka/.

o Kanerika: It leverages AI to enhance quality assurance (QA) processes by automating repetitive tasks, predicting defects before they occur, and offering real-time insights. Specifically, Kanerika can do (1) Automated Testing, automates repetitive testing tasks, including running tests on different scenarios and environments to ensure software quality, allowing QA teams to focus on more complex issues; (2) Defect Prediction, using machine learning models, it analyzes historical data to predict potential defects before they occur; (3) Smart Test Case Generation, it generates test cases based on user behavior and past data, increasing test coverage and uncovering hidden bugs that might otherwise go unnoticed; (4) Real-Time Insights, provides real-time insights into the testing process, helping teams make informed decisions quickly and improve overall efficiency; and (5) Personalized Ad Generation, use generative AI to create highly personalized ads tailored to individual users, improving engagement rates and conversion metrics. You can find more information about Kanerika at kanerika.com.

A couple of AI-driven applications that assess how AI technologies enhance the quality of the product are:

- MLflow is an open-source platform that helps manage the machine learning lifecycle, including experimentation, reproducibility, and deployment. It can track and compare different models' performance metrics, thereby providing insights into how much better one model is compared to another. It helps in assessing the quality improvements of AI models by analyzing their performance over time. You can find out more information on MLflow at mlflow.org.

- Weights & Biases is a tool designed for tracking machine learning experiments. It allows you to visualize and compare different runs, making it easier to see the impact of changes on model performance. It provides detailed analytics and reports on model performance, helping you measure the quality improvements of your AI technologies. You can find out more information on Weights & Biases at wandb.ai.

Ultimately, executives who prioritize accuracy and quality in their AI implementations will be better positioned to achieve sustained success and excellence in their operations.

Customer Experience

In today's competitive landscape, KPIs play a vital role in evaluating and enhancing the customer experience through the lens of AI. By leveraging advanced data analytics and AI-driven insights, executives can gain a deeper understanding of customer behavior, preferences, and satisfaction levels. KPIs such as customer satisfaction scores (CSAT), net promoter scores (NPS), and customer effort scores (CES) provide measurable benchmarks to assess the effectiveness of AI initiatives in improving service quality and customer engagement. Implementing these KPIs helps executives not only optimize their AI strategies but also foster a customer-centric culture that drives continuous improvement and long-term success.[cclxxxix]

Customer Satisfaction Scores

CSAT scores measure customer satisfaction levels after interactions with AI tools. These scores provide insights into how well AI meets customer needs and expectations. AI enhances customer experiences by providing quick and accurate responses, personalized recommendations, and 24/7 support.[ccxc]

A couple of AI-driven platforms that can enhance customer service and satisfaction are:

- Kustomer Assist: It's an advanced AI-powered platform integrated within Kustomer's customer relationship management (CRM) systems. Kustomer Assist enhances customer service operations through intelligent automation, predictive insights, and personalized engagement. It automates various aspects of customer interaction, such as routing conversations to the right agents, automating common responses, and providing real-time guidance during live interactions. You can find more information on Kustomer Assist at kustomer.com.

- Birdeye: It offers AI customer review software that helps organizations manage and analyze customer feedback across multiple platforms, such as online review sites, social media, business listings, customer surveys, and messaging channels. It uses machine learning and natural language processing (NLP) to simplify tasks like feedback analysis, trend detection, and extracting key insights. This helps organizations improve customer satisfaction by providing actionable insights and automating repetitive tasks. You can find more information on Birdeye at birdeye.com.

A couple of AI-enabled software applications that assess CSAT scores are:

- SurveySparrow is a platform that offers automated surveys with real-time insights, allowing organizations to gather and analyze customer feedback efficiently. It provides detailed reports and analytics to help organizations understand customer satisfaction levels and identify areas for improvement. You can find out more information on SurveySparrow at surveysparrow.com.

- Survicate is known for its CSAP surveys and follow-up workflows, enabling organizations to measure customer satisfaction at various touchpoints. It integrates with other tools and provides actionable insights to enhance customer experience. You can find out more information on Survicate at survicate.com.

Net Promoter Score

NPS assesses customer loyalty and their likelihood to recommend the organization. A high NPS indicates that customers are satisfied with their experiences and likely to promote the organization to others. AI can influence NPS by enhancing the overall customer journey, from initial contact to post-purchase support.[ccxci]

A couple of AI-driven platforms that assess NPS are:

- Yellow.ai: It offers a comprehensive solution that automates survey distribution, gathers feedback, and calculates scores. Yellow.ai provides advanced analytics and reporting features to help businesses segment customers, spot trends, and make data-driven decisions to improve customer satisfaction and loyalty. You can find more information on Yellow.ai at yellow.ai.

- Qualaroo: It provides an easy-to-use NPS survey tool that allows organizations to quickly create and send out surveys. Qualaroo offers real-time tracking, customizable campaigns, and in-app surveys to gather honest customer feedback. Its analytics help organizations understand customer sentiment and identify areas for improvement. You can find more information on Qualaroo at qualaroo.com.

Customer Effort Score

CES is a metric used to measure the ease of customer interactions with an organization's products or services. It focuses on the effort a customer has to exert to get an issue resolved, a request fulfilled, or a service provided. The goal of CES is to minimize the effort required for customers to have their needs met, thereby improving overall customer satisfaction and loyalty.[ccxcii]

Here's an example of how it works:

- Survey Question: Typically, CES is measured using a survey question such as, "How easy was it to resolve your issue?" Customers respond on a scale (e.g., from "Very Difficult" to "Very Easy").

- Scoring: Responses are then aggregated to provide an overall CES score, which helps the organization identify areas where customers face the most friction.

- Improvement: By analyzing CES data, organizations can pinpoint and address pain points in their customer service processes, ultimately striving to make interactions smoother and more efficient.

CES is valuable because it highlights the importance of reducing customer effort, which is often a key driver of customer loyalty and satisfaction.[ccxciii]

A couple of AI-enabled platforms that measure CES are:

- Frame AI: It offers intelligent AI models designed to quantify customer effort and reduce friction in customer interactions. Frame AI provides real-time insights into friction points across various interactions, such as long wait times, multiple interactions with multiple departments by the customer, customers struggling to navigate a website or application, and slow response times to customer inquiries when customers are required to follow-up via different channels like email after a phone call, helping teams to reduce customer effort and improve overall satisfaction. Some of the features include effort scores, risk alerts, issue resolution tracking, and multi-channel synthesis. You can find more information on Frame AI at frame.ai.

- Retently: It provides tools specifically for measuring CES and customer satisfaction. Retently helps organizations understand how easy or difficult it is for customers to interact with their services and identifies areas where effort can be reduced and, thus, customer satisfaction improved. Retently includes CES surveys, real-time feedback, and advanced analytics to help businesses improve their customer journey. You can find more information on Retently at retently.com.

Response Times

Response times measure how quickly AI-powered solutions address customer inquiries and support requests. Faster response times lead to higher customer satisfaction as customers appreciate quick and efficient service. AI chatbots and virtual assistants handle inquiries instantly, providing customers with immediate assistance regardless of the number of inquiries at one time.[ccxciv]

A couple of AI-driven platforms to automate customer interactions are:

- Zendesk: Its AI-powered features, such as Answer Bot and Smart Chat, help reduce response times by automating responses to common customer queries and intelligently routing more complex issues to human agents. This ensures that customers receive timely and accurate support. It has the capability to measure and assess how quickly it addresses customer inquiries and support requests. You can find more information on Zendesk at zendesk.com.

- LivePerson: Its Conversational Cloud uses AI to automate customer interactions across various platforms, including websites, social media, and mobile devices. It helps organizations respond quickly to customer inquiries by routing messages to the right agents and providing real-time guidance during live interactions. It also has the capabilities to measure and assess how quickly it addresses customer inquiries and support requests You can find more information on LivePerson at liveperson.com.

By incorporating these KPIs, executives can not only harness the power of AI to elevate the customer experience but also create a sustainable competitive edge that supports ongoing growth and customer loyalty.

Adoption and Utilization

In the realm of AI, KPIs for adoption and utilization are essential metrics that help measure the effectiveness and integration of AI solutions within an organization. These KPIs provide valuable insights into how widely AI tools are being adopted, the frequency of their use, and the overall impact on organizational processes and outcomes. By tracking metrics such as user engagement, adoption rates, and utilization frequency, executives can identify areas for improvement, drive better adoption strategies, and ensure that AI technologies are delivering the desired value. Most AI solutions include tools to measure user engagement, adoption rate, and usage frequency. Understanding and optimizing these KPIs is crucial for maximizing the return on investment (ROI) and achieving long-term success with AI implementations.[ccxcv] Leveraging analytics platforms, performance metrics, and A/B testing is essential for accurately measuring these KPIs, thereby enabling organizations to make data-driven decisions and continuously refine their AI strategies to maximize effectiveness and ROI.[ccxcvi]

Analytics Platforms

Analytics platforms serve as the foundation for transforming raw data into actionable insights, enabling executives to leverage data-driven strategies to drive growth and innovation.[ccxcvii]

- AI Dashboards: AI dashboards provide real-time insights into AI performance metrics and KPIs, which can be tailored to track specific organizational goals. By visualizing data in a user-friendly way, these dashboards help stakeholders make informed decisions. For example, an AI dashboard might track metrics such as algorithm accuracy, processing speed, error rates, and customer satisfaction scores, providing a holistic view of the AI system's impact on business operations.[ccxcviii]

The following are a couple of AI dashboard platforms:

  o Lazy AI Dashboard: This platform offers various templates for AI dashboards, including social-media performance tracking, admin dashboards, and machine learning model evaluation. It provides real-time insights and performance metrics to help organizations optimize their operations and marketing campaigns. You can find out more information about Lazy AI Dashboard at getlazy.ai.

  o Qlik Dashboard: Qlik provides a range of AI-powered dashboards tailored to different industries and roles. Their dashboards integrate data from multiple sources, such as databases, spreadsheets, could services, SaaS applications, data warehouses, application programming interfaces (APIs), and streaming data, offering actionable predictions and insights to drive business outcomes. They also support predictive and generative AI to help organizations make smarter decisions. You can find out more information on Qlik at qlik.com.

- Data Visualization Tools: Data visualization tools are essential for transforming raw data into interactive and visually engaging formats. These tools can integrate with AI systems to display performance metrics such as trends over time, anomaly detection, and predictive analytics. The visual representation of data through charts, graphs, and maps helps executives quickly identify patterns, outliers, and opportunities for improvement.[ccxcix] The following are a couple of data visualization tools:

  o Tableau: It's a leading data visualization tool known for its user-friendly interface and powerful capabilities. It allows users to create a wide range of interactive and shareable dashboards with some of its key features, including a drag-and-drop interface, data connectivity, interactive dashboards, advanced analytics, and the ability to collaborate. You can find more information on Tableau at tableau.com.

  o Power BI: It's a data visualization and business intelligence tool developed by Microsoft. It integrates seamlessly with other Microsoft products and offers robust features like data connectivity, interactive reports, natural language queries, real-time dashboards, and AI-powered insights. You can find more information on Power BI at powerbi.com.

Performance Metrics

Performance metrics serve as essential tools for evaluating the effectiveness and efficiency of various processes within an organization, providing data-driven insights to inform strategic decisions.[ccc]

- Precision and Recall: Precision measures the number of true positive results divided by the number of true positive and false positive results. It answers the question, "Of all the items identified as relevant, how many were actually relevant?" Recall, on the other hand, measures the number of true positive results divided by the number of true positive and false negative results. It answers: "Of all the relevant items, how many were identified?" These metrics are crucial for tasks such as spam detection, where precision ensures that non-spam emails are rarely marked as spam, and recall ensures that most spam emails are caught.[ccci]

  o Precision = $\dfrac{\text{True Positives}}{\text{(True Positives + False Positives)}}$ Recall = $\dfrac{\text{True Positives}}{\text{(True Positives + False Negatives)}}$

The following are a couple of AI platforms that can provide precision and recall metrics:

- o Evidently: The open-source Python library offers tools to calculate and visualize various classification metrics, including precision and recall. It's particularly useful for evaluating the performance of machine learning models. You can find more information on Evidently at evidentlyai.com.

- o Julius.ai: This platform provides a comprehensive suite of tools for evaluating machine learning models, including precision and recall metrics. It helps in understanding model performance, especially in classification tasks. You can find more information on Julius AI at julius.ai.

- F1 Score: The F1 score is the harmonic mean of precision and recall, providing a single metric that balances both concerns. It's particularly useful in situations where an even balance between precision and recall is desired. The F1 score is calculated as:

$$F1 = 2 \text{ x } \frac{\text{(Precision x Recall)}}{\text{(Precision + Recall)}}$$

This metric is valuable in scenarios like medical diagnostics, where both false positives and false negatives can have significant consequences.[cccii]

The following are a couple of platforms that can calculate the FI score:

- o Scikit-learn: This popular Python library offers functions to calculate the FI Score and related metrics, as well as tools for cross-validation and model selection based on these metrics. You can find more information on Scikit-learn at skikit-learn.org.
- o Julius.ai: This platform provides a comprehensive suite of tools for evaluating machine learning models, including F1 Score. It helps in understanding model performance, especially in classification tasks. You can find more information on Julius AI at julius.ai.

- Confusion Matrix: A confusion matrix is a table used to evaluate the performance of a classification model. It summarizes the results of predictions, showing the number of true positives (correctly predicted positives), true negatives (correctly predicted negatives), false positives (incorrectly predicted positives), and false negatives (incorrectly predicted negatives). Analyzing the confusion matrix helps identify specific areas where the model excels or needs improvement, such as high false positive rates indicating over-classification of certain categories.[ccciii]

The following are a couple of platforms that can create confusion matrix visuals:

o MyMap.AI: This platform has an AI-powered confusion matrix maker that allows you to create visual confusion matrices by simply uploading your classification data. It provides real-time insights and performance metrics for evaluating machine learning models. You can find more information on MyMap.AI at mymap.ai.

o Nyckel: Nyckel provides a confusion matrix creator that generates confusion matrices from CSV files containing actual and predicted labels. It visualizes the accuracy of your classification model and helps identify areas for improvement. You can find more information on Nyckel at nyckel.com.

A/B Testing

A/B testing is a crucial experimental approach used to compare two versions of a product, feature, process, system, or campaign to determine which one performs better based on specific metrics and user behavior analysis.[ccciv]

• Control vs. Experimental Groups: In AI, this can mean comparing an AI-driven process with a traditional, non-AI process. For example, an online retailer might use A/B testing to compare the effectiveness of an AI-driven recommendation engine against a human-curated list. By analyzing metrics like click-through rates, conversion rates, and customer satisfaction, the retailer can quantify the improvement brought by the AI system.[cccv]

The following are a couple of platforms that have AI-driven A/B testing capabilities:

- o Kameleoon: This platform offers AI-driven A/B testing capabilities, allowing organizations to run experiments and analyze results more efficiently. It leverages generative and predictive AI to optimize test designs and improve decision-making. You can find more information on Kameleoon at kameleoon.com.

- o Looppanel: It integrates AI tools like ChatGPT to make A/B testing faster and more effective. It helps organizations generate test ideas, analyze data in real time, and identify winning variations quickly. You can find more information on Looppanel at looppanel.com.

- Conversion Rates: Conversion rates measure the percentage of users who take a desired action, such as making a purchase, signing up for a newsletter, or completing a survey. By comparing conversion rates between control and experimental groups, executives can assess the impact of AI on achieving specific organizational goals. Higher conversion rates in the experimental group suggest that the AI-driven approach is more effective in driving desired outcomes.[cccvi]

The following are a couple of platforms that calculate conversion rates and compare the conversion rates between control and experimental groups so executives can assess the impact of AI on achieving specific organizational goals:

o Google Analytics: This powerful tool allows organizations to set up experiments and compare conversion rates between different versions of a webpage or campaign. It provides detailed reports and insights to help assess the impact of the changes. You can find more information on Google Analytics at gooogle.com/analytics.

o Optimizely: It offers A/B testing and personalization features that enable organizations to run experiments and compare conversion rates between control and experimental groups. It helps in understanding the effectiveness of different variations and making data-driven decisions. You can find more information on Optimizely at developers.optimizely.com.

Thus, by prioritizing the measurement and optimization of these KPIs, executives can fully harness the potential of AI technologies, thereby driving innovation and achieving a sustained competitive advantage.

Continuous Improvement and Iteration in AI Projects

Executives should always strive for continuous improvement and iteration as they are vital to maintaining the relevance and effectiveness of the organizations' AI projects. This section shares some of the strategies and practices that drive ongoing enhancements, ensuring AI systems are adaptable, resilient, and capable of delivering optimal results. Although we will touch upon the importance of feedback loops, regular model retraining, and benchmarking against industry standards, it's important to note that these functions are usually performed by an organization's AI/ML Project or Product Manager or a Data Scientist or Machine Learning Engineer. Nevertheless, executives should be aware of what they are so that they can make sure these iterative processes are properly implemented and not only refine the organization's AI performance but pave the way for sustained success and a competitive advantage in an increasingly data-driven world.

Feedback Loops

In AI, feedback loops refer to the processes where the system's outputs are fed back as inputs to adjust and improve the system's performance over time, enabling continuous learning and optimization.[cccvii] They can play a critical role in refining AI systems by continuously incorporating user input and performance data to drive iterative improvements and optimizations. Executives should utilize feedback loops within their organizations to refine their AI systems.[cccviii]

Model Retraining

Model training in AI involves feeding data to an algorithm to enable it to learn patterns and make predictions or decisions based on that data.[cccix] Therefore, model retraining, including regular updates, adaptive learning mechanisms, and continuous evaluation, can be vital for your organization's AI models as it enables you to stay current with evolving data, maintain accuracy, and adapt to new challenges and opportunities.[cccx]

Incremental Development

Incremental development in AI refers to the continuous and adaptive process of updating AI models with new data, allowing them to learn and improve over time without forgetting previously acquired knowledge.[cccxi] Embarking on any AI project within an organization requires meticulous planning and methodical execution to ensure success. Executives should employ their organization's data scientist, machine learning engineer, or AI/ML project or product manager to implement comprehensive testing and run controlled pilot programs so that they can refine their AI solutions, mitigate risks, and ultimately drive innovation and value in the fast-evolving field of AI. Incremental development is especially a critical approach in software development.[cccxii]

Benchmarking and Best Practices

Benchmarking and best practices in AI involve evaluating AI systems against industry standards and proven methodologies to ensure optimal performance, efficiency, and continuous improvement. Benchmarking and adopting best practices are essential components in driving the success of AI projects within an organization.

By leveraging industry benchmarks, executives can conduct comparative analyses and identify both the strengths and weaknesses in its AI initiatives, ensuring continuous improvement and alignment with industry standards. Regularly updating benchmarks and performance goals fosters a culture of striving for excellence. Meanwhile, learning from successes, documenting knowledge, and sharing best practices promote a culture of continuous learning and innovation within the organization. Together, these practices enable executives to refine methodologies, optimize workflows, and adopt the latest technological advancements.[cccxiii]

In summary, the success of AI initiatives within an organization hinges on a holistic approach to measurement that integrates both quantitative and qualitative metrics. By thoughtfully defining success criteria, continually refining processes based on real-time feedback, and fostering a culture of adaptability, executives can navigate the complex landscape of AI with confidence and precision. As AI technologies evolve, so too must strategies for assessing their value. By prioritizing alignment with organizational objectives and maintaining a relentless focus on outcomes, executives can not only unlock the full potential of their AI investments but also drive innovation and sustainable growth in an ever-changing world.

Chapter 12:
The Road Ahead For AI

As we stand at the forefront of this new technological era, the landscape of AI is ripe for amazing and groundbreaking advancements that will have monumental impacts across a multitude of sectors. This chapter will examine the emerging trends and future directions that will shape the AI journey ahead. From the promise of quantum computing to the democratization of AI literacy, this chapter illuminates the path forward, offering insights into the preparations required for harnessing the full potential of AI in driving innovation and fostering a more inclusive and sustainable future.

Emerging Trends and Future Directions in AI

Emerging trends and cutting-edge advancements are paving the way for unprecedented capabilities and applications across various sectors. From the revolutionary integration of quantum computing to the rise of edge AI, these developments are set to redefine the boundaries of what's possible with AI. Let's explore the AI technologies and practices that will shape the future and unlock new opportunities for growth, efficiency, and societal impact.[cccxiv]

Advancements in AI Technology

In recent years, significant advancements in AI technology have been driving remarkable innovations and transforming various industries.

AI and Quantum Computing:

Quantum computing leverages quantum bits, or qubits, which can exist in multiple states simultaneously, allowing for parallel processing of vast amounts of data. The integration of AI with quantum computing promises to revolutionize fields such as cryptography, optimization, and complex simulations. For example, in cryptography, quantum AI could break encryption algorithms that are currently considered secure, necessitating the development of quantum-resistant cryptographic techniques. In optimization, quantum AI could solve problems related to logistics, supply chain management, and financial modeling more efficiently, thereby leading to significant cost savings and operational improvements. Moreover, quantum simulations could lead to breakthroughs in material science, enabling the discovery of new materials with unique properties for various applications, from electronics to pharmaceuticals.[cccxv]

Edge AI:

Edge AI is the practice of running AI algorithms directly on devices at the "edge" of the network rather than relying on a centralized cloud infrastructure. This means that data is processed and analyzed closer to where it's generated, such as smartphones and IoT devices, rather than being sent to remote data centers.[cccxvi]

Edge AI brings the power of AI closer to the data source, such as the Internet of Things (IoT) devices, sensors, and smart cameras, reducing the need for constant communication with centralized cloud servers. This proximity enables faster processing times, lower latency, and improved real-time decision-making capabilities. For example, in AVs, edge AI can process sensor data locally to make split-second decisions, ensuring safety and efficiency on the road. In smart cities, edge AI can analyze data from various sensors to optimize traffic flow, reduce energy consumption, and enhance public safety. Furthermore, edge AI can improve the performance of wearable devices, enabling advanced health monitoring and personalized fitness recommendations.[cccxvii]

Explainable AI (XAI):

Explainable AI (XAI) aims to provide transparent and interpretable AI models that can offer clear explanations for their decisions and actions. This transparency is crucial for building trust and accountability, especially in high-stakes domains such as healthcare, finance, and legal systems. For example, in healthcare, XAI can help doctors understand the reasoning behind AI-generated diagnoses and treatment recommendations, thereby allowing them to make more informed decisions and build trust with patients. In finance, XAI can provide explanations for credit scoring and loan approval decisions, reducing the risk of bias and discrimination. Moreover, XAI can facilitate regulatory compliance by providing clear documentation of AI decision-making processes, ensuring that organizations adhere to ethical guidelines and standards.[cccxviii]

AI in Emerging Industries

AI is set to revolutionize a myriad of emerging industries, bringing advancements that promise to reshape the landscape of innovation and productivity. From biotechnology and healthcare to environmental sustainability and creative fields, AI is unlocking new possibilities and addressing complex challenges with unprecedented precision and efficiency. Let's explore the profound potential impact of AI across some dynamic sectors, highlighting its transformative potential.[cccxix]

AI in Biotechnology and Healthcare

AI is revolutionizing biotechnology and healthcare by accelerating drug discovery, enabling personalized medicine, and advancing genomics research. AI algorithms can analyze massive datasets of biological information to identify potential therapeutic targets, predict patient responses to treatments, and optimize clinical trial designs. For example, AI can help researchers discover new drugs by analyzing the molecular structures of compounds and predicting their efficacy and safety profiles. In personalized medicine, AI can tailor treatment plans based on individual genetic profiles, improving patient outcomes and minimizing side effects. Additionally, AI-driven tools can assist in early diagnosis and disease monitoring, enabling timely interventions and better management of chronic conditions.[cccxx]

AI in Environmental Sustainability

AI technologies have the potential to address pressing environmental challenges by optimizing resource usage, reducing waste, and monitoring climate change on a large scale. In agriculture, AI-driven innovations such as precision farming and smart irrigation systems can enhance crop yields while minimizing environmental impact. For example, AI can analyze soil data, weather patterns, and satellite imagery to provide farmers with actionable insights on optimal planting times, irrigation schedules, and pest management strategies.[cccxxi] In energy management, AI can optimize the performance of renewable energy sources like solar panels and wind turbines, thus improving efficiency and reducing costs.[cccxxii] Moreover, AI can help monitor and predict the effects of climate change by analyzing vast datasets of environmental information, enabling better policy decisions and mitigation strategies.[cccxxiii]

AI in Creative Industries

AI is making significant inroads into creative fields, pushing the boundaries of what is possible in art, music, and literature. AI-generated content, such as paintings, music compositions, and written works, is becoming increasingly sophisticated, challenging traditional notions of creativity. For example, AI algorithms can generate original artwork by analyzing existing pieces and creating new compositions that blend different styles and techniques.[cccxxiv] In music, AI can compose melodies, harmonize arrangements, and even generate lyrics, providing musicians with new tools for creative collaboration.[cccxxv] In literature, AI can assist writers by generating plot ideas, suggesting character developments, and enhancing writing styles. As AI continues to evolve, it will open up new possibilities for creative expression and collaboration, enriching the cultural landscape.[cccxxvi]

The relentless march of AI across these dynamic sectors not only signals a new era of innovation but also heralds a future where technology and human ingenuity intertwine to solve the world's most pressing challenges.

Possible New AI Uses for Organizations

Let's look at some of the possible new AI uses for organizations in the not-so-far future:

1. Sensory Augmentation Devices: AI could be integrated into wearables that enhance human senses, such as amplifying hearing, improving night vision, or even detecting odors, giving users a superhuman sensory experience.[cccxxvii]

2. Dynamic Workspaces: AI could manage and adapt physical office environments in real time to optimize productivity and well-being. This includes adjusting lighting, temperature, and layout based on employees' needs and preferences.[cccxxviii]

3. Interactive Storytelling Experiences: AI could create immersive, interactive narratives for entertainment or educational purposes. Users could engage in real time with characters and storylines that adapt based on their choices and behavior.[cccxxix]

4. Emotionally Aware Virtual Assistants: AI could develop virtual assistants capable of understanding and responding to human emotions, providing empathetic support and personalized interactions in customer service, healthcare, and personal applications.[cccxxx]

5. AI-Driven Urban Planning: AI could assist in designing smart cities by analyzing vast amounts of data to optimize traffic flow, reduce pollution, and enhance public safety, creating more efficient and sustainable urban environments.[cccxxxi]

6. Mind-Machine Interfaces (MMIs): AI could be used to develop interfaces that allow humans to control devices using their thoughts. This could revolutionize fields such as accessibility, gaming, and communication.[cccxxxii]

7. Personalized Retail Experiences: AI could create virtual shopping assistants that provide personalized recommendations, styling advice, and interactive experiences based on a shopper's preferences and past behaviors.[cccxxxiii]

8. AI-Enhanced Collaborative Creativity: AI could facilitate creative collaboration between individuals and teams, generating new ideas and solutions in fields like advertising, product design, and innovation.[cccxxxiv]

9. AI-Powered Memory Enhancement: AI could assist individuals in enhancing their memory and cognitive abilities by providing personalized brain training exercises, monitoring cognitive health, and offering real-time feedback.[cccxxxv]

These are just the tip of the iceberg when it comes to the untapped potential of AI, as the future holds endless possibilities for how AI can revolutionize various industries and improve our lives in ways we have yet to imagine.

Ethical and Regulatory Considerations

As the influence and capabilities of AI continue to expand, it becomes increasingly crucial to address the ethical and regulatory considerations that accompany its development and deployment. Ensuring that AI technologies are used responsibly and transparently is crucial to building trust and safeguarding societal values.[cccxxxvi]

AI Ethics and Governance

As AI technology advances, there will be a greater focus on establishing ethical guidelines and governance frameworks to ensure responsible development and use of AI. This includes addressing issues such as fairness, accountability, transparency, and bias in AI systems. For example, organizations may implement ethical review boards to oversee AI projects and ensure that they adhere to ethical standards. Governments and regulatory bodies may develop policies and regulations to guide the ethical use of AI, balancing innovation with societal values and human rights. Moreover, there will be a growing emphasis on inclusive and participatory approaches to AI governance, involving diverse stakeholders in decision-making processes to ensure that AI benefits all members of society.[cccxxxvii]

Privacy and Data Security

As AI develops and advances, executives must continue to adapt to it and ensure that they have proper and necessary robust privacy and data security measures in place.

Bias Mitigation

Addressing biases in AI algorithms will be a major area of focus, as biased AI systems can perpetuate and exacerbate existing inequalities. Efforts to develop unbiased and fair AI systems will drive research and policy-making, including the development of techniques for detecting and mitigating biases in AI models. For example, researchers may develop algorithms that can identify and correct biases in training data, thus ensuring that AI systems make fair and equitable decisions. Policymakers may establish guidelines and regulations to promote fairness and accountability in AI, such as requiring regular audits of AI systems to identify and address potential biases. Furthermore, executives may implement best practices for diversity and inclusion in AI development, ensuring that AI systems reflect the values and perspectives of diverse communities.[cccxxxviii]

Navigating the ethical and regulatory landscape of AI is crucial to fostering responsible development and deployment of AI technologies. By addressing ethical challenges such as bias, privacy, accountability, and staying abreast of and adhering to evolving regulatory frameworks, executives can ensure that their AI systems are transparent, fair, and aligned with societal values.

Preparing for the Next Major Wave of AI Technological Advancements

As we stand on the brink of the next major wave of AI technological advancements, the need for strategic preparation and proactive adaptation has never been more critical for executives. The rapid pace of innovation promises groundbreaking developments that will transform industries, redefine job roles, and reshape our everyday lives. To fully harness the potential of these advancements, it's essential for executives to focus on education and skill development, investment in AI research and development, and infrastructure investment.

Education and Skill Development

Education and skill development are crucial in equipping individuals and organizations with the knowledge and capabilities needed to adapt to and thrive amidst the rapid advancements and transformative potential of AI technology and can be accomplished by ensuring AI literacy for everyone, developing advanced training programs, and encouraging interdisciplinary collaboration.

AI Literacy for All:

Promoting AI literacy across various sectors will be essential for ensuring that individuals and organizations can harness the full potential of AI. This includes integrating AI education into school curriculums, providing accessible learning resources for the general public, and offering training programs for professionals. For example, schools may introduce AI concepts and hands-on projects to students at an early age, fostering a foundational understanding of AI technologies. Public libraries and online platforms may offer free AI courses and workshops, making AI education accessible to a broader audience. Moreover, organizations may provide AI training programs for their employees, helping them develop the skills needed to work with AI technologies and drive innovation within their industries.[cccxxxix]

Advanced Training Programs:

Developing specialized training programs for professionals to acquire advanced AI skills will be crucial for meeting the demands of the rapidly evolving AI landscape. This includes courses in machine learning, data science, AI ethics, and other related fields. For example, universities and training institutions may offer advanced degree programs and certifications in AI, providing professionals with the ability to acquire in-depth knowledge and expertise. Organizations may partner with academic institutions to develop tailored training programs that address industry-specific needs and challenges. Furthermore, professional organizations and industry associations may offer continuing education opportunities to ensure that professionals stay up-to-date with the latest advancements in AI.[cccxl]

Interdisciplinary Collaboration:

Encouraging collaboration between AI experts and professionals from other fields, such as healthcare, law, and the arts, will be essential for fostering innovative solutions that address complex societal challenges. For example, interdisciplinary research teams may work together to develop AI-powered medical devices that improve patient outcomes or AI-driven legal tools that enhance access to justice. Collaborative projects may also bring together artists and technologists to explore new forms of creative expression and cultural production. By fostering interdisciplinary collaboration, we can leverage the diverse perspectives and expertise of different fields to drive innovation and address the upcoming challenges of the future.[cccxli]

Ultimately, by prioritizing education and skill development, executives can create a future where AI technology is leveraged responsibly and effectively to benefit all facets of society.

Investment in AI Research and Development

Investment in AI research and development from public and private funding ensures that we are well-prepared to navigate and lead the next wave of transformative advancements, and promoting collaborative research initiatives will be crucial for accelerating AI advancements.

Public and Private Funding:

Increasing investment in AI research and development from both the public and private sectors will be essential for driving innovation and commercialization of AI technologies. This includes funding initiatives that focus on cutting-edge research, technological innovation, and the development of AI applications that address societal challenges. For example, governments may allocate funds for AI research grants and innovation programs, supporting universities, research institutions, and startups in their efforts to develop groundbreaking AI technologies. Private companies and venture capital firms may invest in AI startups and projects, providing the financial resources needed to bring innovative AI solutions to market. Moreover, philanthropic organizations and foundations may support AI research and initiatives that aim to address global challenges, such as clean water, healthcare, and education.[cccxlii]

Collaborative Research Initiatives:

Promoting collaborative research initiatives between academia, industry, and government will be crucial for accelerating AI advancements and addressing complex societal challenges. For example, public-private partnerships may facilitate the sharing of resources, expertise, and data, thereby enabling researchers to tackle large-scale AI projects more effectively. Collaborative research centers and consortia may bring together researchers from different institutions and disciplines to work on common AI challenges and opportunities. Furthermore, international collaborations may foster the exchange of knowledge and best practices, thus advancing AI research and development on a global scale.[cccxliii]

By embracing a unified approach and fostering strong partnerships, executives can harness the full potential of AI, drive innovation, and create a future where technology serves the greater good.

Infrastructure and Ecosystem Development

Investing in a strong infrastructure and fostering a resilient AI ecosystem ensures that the upcoming wave of AI technological advancements can be seamlessly integrated, effectively managed, and widely beneficial. Moreover, supporting AI startups and innovation hubs, as well as establishing regulatory sandboxes, will ensure that AI is developed responsibly and sustainably.

AI Infrastructure:

Developing robust AI infrastructure, including high-performance computing resources, data centers, and cloud platforms, will be essential for supporting large-scale AI applications. For example, governments and private companies may invest in the development of state-of-the-art AI research facilities, thereby providing researchers with access to the computational power needed to train and deploy advanced AI models. Cloud service providers may offer scalable AI platforms that enable organizations to harness the power of AI without the need for significant upfront investments in infrastructure. Furthermore, developing open-source AI frameworks and tools can foster innovation and collaboration within the AI community, helping to drive the development of new AI applications and solutions.[cccxliv]

Startups and Innovation Hubs:

Supporting AI startups and innovation hubs will be crucial for fostering entrepreneurship and driving AI-driven economic growth. Incubators and accelerators can play a vital role in nurturing innovative AI solutions by providing startups with the resources, mentorship, and funding needed to bring their ideas to market. Governments and private organizations may establish innovation hubs and tech parks that create collaborative environments for AI startups, researchers, and industry professionals to work together and share ideas. Moreover, initiatives that promote knowledge transfer and collaboration between established companies and startups can accelerate the commercialization of AI technologies and drive economic growth.[cccxlv]

Regulatory Sandboxes:

Establishing regulatory sandboxes where AI innovations can be tested in a controlled environment before full-scale deployment will help to ensure that AI technologies are developed and used responsibly. Regulatory sandboxes allow for experimentation and innovation while ensuring compliance with regulatory standards and mitigating potential risks. For example, governments may create sandbox environments for testing AI applications in healthcare, finance, and autonomous systems, allowing developers to first assess the safety, efficacy, and ethical implications of their technologies. By providing a structured framework for innovation, regulatory sandboxes can help balance the need for technological advancement with the protection of public interests and values.[cccxlvi]

In summary, the impending wave of AI technological advancements presents both immense opportunities and significant challenges for organizations and their executives. By strategically preparing and proactively adapting to these changes, executives can unlock the full potential of AI and drive innovation, efficiency, and growth. Focusing on education and skill development will help to ensure that the workforce remains agile and capable, while investment in AI research and development will foster cutting-edge solutions. Furthermore, robust infrastructure investment is critical to support the seamless integration of AI technologies.

Final Thoughts and Reflections

As we conclude our exploration of AI and its impact on organizations, it's essential to reflect on the profound transformations this technology has catalyzed across various domains. AI has not only revolutionized industries and enhanced our daily lives. In these final thoughts, we will discuss the lessons learned, the opportunities that lie ahead, and the responsibilities executives bear in harnessing AI's potential. By contemplating the journey so far and the future trajectory, we can better understand how to navigate the complex AI landscape.

The Transformative Potential of AI

AI has the transformative potential to revolutionize industries, enhance human capabilities, and drive unprecedented innovation across numerous sectors. AI has the capability to empower humanity but will require collaboration, a diverse approach, and continuous learning and adaptation along the way.

Empowering Humanity:

AI has the potential to empower humanity by augmenting human capabilities, improving decision-making, and enhancing the quality of life. By leveraging AI technologies responsibly, executives can address some of the world's most pressing challenges, from healthcare and education to sustainable energy and economic development. Embracing AI with a focus on both ethical principles and societal benefits can lead to significant advancements that improve the well-being of individuals and communities worldwide.[cccxlvii]

Collaboration and Inclusivity:

The future of AI will require collaboration across disciplines, industries, and borders. Inclusive and diverse approaches to AI development will ensure that AI benefits all of humanity and addresses global challenges equitably. By fostering interdisciplinary collaboration and engaging diverse stakeholders in the AI development process, executives can create innovative solutions that reflect the values and needs of different communities. Collaboration between governments, industry, academia, and civil society will also be essential for shaping the future of AI in a way that promotes inclusivity, fairness, and shared prosperity.[cccxlviii]

Continuous Learning and Adaptation:

The AI landscape is constantly evolving, and continuous learning and adaptation will be crucial for executives, organizations as a whole, and societies to stay ahead of technological advancements. By fostering a culture of lifelong learning and embracing change, we can equip ourselves with the knowledge and skills needed to harness the full potential that AI has to offer. Executives must invest in upskilling their workforce and developing agile strategies that allow them to adapt to the rapidly changing AI ecosystem. Executives must also remain curious and open to new opportunities, continuously seeking to learn, understand, and leverage AI technologies in both their professional and personal lives.[cccxlix]

In conclusion, the future of AI holds boundless potential and exciting opportunities. By reflecting on the journey thus far and advancing forward with a steadfast commitment to collaboration, ethical principles, and continuous learning, we can unlock the transformative power of AI. This will enable us to drive innovation, tackle societal challenges, and create a sustainable future for all. Together, we can shape an AI-enabled world that embodies our highest values and aspirations, ensuring that the benefits of this amazing technology are equitably shared and thoughtfully applied.

Epilogue

As we stand on the cusp of an AI-driven revolution, it's imperative for executives to embrace and harness the transformative power of AI. Throughout this book, we've explored the intricate interplay between AI and leadership, delving into the strategies, tools, and mindsets necessary to thrive in this new era. The insights gleaned from AI-powered leadership are not merely theoretical but practical and actionable, offering a blueprint for navigating the complexities of the modern business landscape.

AI is not just a tool but a catalyst for change; it challenges us to rethink traditional models, question established norms, and innovate beyond the conventional. Executives who understand this paradigm shift and are willing to adapt will find themselves at the forefront of industry advancements.

However, the journey doesn't end here. As AI continues to evolve, so too must our approaches and understanding. Executives who remain adaptable, forward-thinking, and ethically grounded will not only lead their organizations to new heights but will also contribute to a more innovative, inclusive, and prosperous future. The responsibility of wielding AI with wisdom and integrity cannot be overstated. Ethical considerations, transparency, and accountability must be at the core of all AI-driven decisions to ensure that the technology benefits everyone.

Remember, the true power of AI lies not just in its algorithms and data but in how we, as leaders, choose to wield it for the betterment of our organizations and society at large. The future of AI-powered leadership is bright, and the onus is on each of us to shape it with wisdom, vision, and integrity. Be sure to continuously strive to learn, as Sophia Bush put it so elegantly, "You are allowed to both a masterpiece and a work in progress simultaneously."

The era of AI-powered leadership is just beginning, and the possibilities are boundless. Let us embark on this journey with confidence, curiosity, and a steadfast dedication to making a positive impact. Together, we can redefine the future of executive leadership and create a world where technology and humanity work hand in hand to achieve greatness.

Key Responsibilities of the AI-Enabled CEO

Being an AI-enabled CEO is an exciting and challenging role that requires a blend of technical knowledge, strategic vision, and leadership skills. Here are some key areas to focus on:

Strategic Vision and Leadership

- Define the Mission and Vision: Clearly articulate your organization's mission and vision, focusing on how AI can drive innovation and create value for customers and stakeholders.
- Set Goals and Objectives: Establish short-term and long-term goals that align with your organization's mission and vision and ensure these goals are objectively measurable and achievable.
- Lead by Example: Demonstrate strong leadership qualities, including integrity, transparency, and a commitment to ethical practices, including those pertinent to AI.

Technical Knowledge and Innovation

- Stay Updated: Keep abreast of the latest developments in AI technology, including exciting new platforms, machine learning, natural language processing, and computer vision.

- Foster Innovation: Encourage a culture of innovation within your organization and support research and development initiatives as well as invest in cutting-edge technologies.
- Collaborate with Experts: Work closely with AI researchers, data scientists, engineers, and other experts to understand the technical aspects of AI and their potential beneficial applications in your organization.

Ethical AI Practices

- Promote Ethical AI: Ensure that your organization's AI solutions are developed and deployed ethically and address issues such as bias, fairness, and transparency in your AI systems.
- Data Protection: Implement with your general counsel and IT department robust data protection measures to safeguard user data and comply with all relevant data and privacy regulations.
- Transparency: Be transparent about how AI is used within your organization and how it impacts customers and stakeholders.

Business Strategy and Operations

- Market Analysis: Conduct a thorough market analysis to identify opportunities and threats (SWOT). Thoroughly understand the competitive landscape and position of your organization accordingly.

- Product Development: Oversee the development of products and services that meet customer needs and provide a competitive advantage.

- Operational Efficiency: Streamline operations to improve efficiency and reduce costs. Always implement best practices in project management and quality control.

Customer and Stakeholder Engagement

- Customer Focus: Prioritize customer satisfaction by delivering high-quality solutions and providing excellent customer support.

- Stakeholder Communication: Maintain open lines of communication with stakeholders, including investors, employees, and customers. Keep them informed about your organization's progress and future plans.

- Partnerships and Collaborations: Build strategic partnerships with other organizations, research institutions, and industry organizations to drive growth and innovation.

Financial Management

- Budgeting and Forecasting: Develop and manage the organization's budget. Forecast financial performance and make data-driven decisions to ensure financial stability.

- Fundraising: Secure funding from financial institutions, investors, and venture capitalists to support the company's growth and expansion.
- Financial Reporting: Ensure accurate and timely financial reporting. Monitor key financial metrics on a regular basis and take corrective actions when necessary.

Top Talent Management

- Attract and Retain Talent: Hire top talent for your C-level executives as well as other key leadership roles in your organization. Create a positive work environment that fosters employee engagement and retention.
- Training and Development: Invest in employee training and development programs to enhance their skills and knowledge.
- Diversity and Inclusion: Promote diversity and inclusion within your organization and ensure that all employees have equal opportunities for growth and advancement.

Regulatory Compliance

- Understand Regulations: Stay informed about all relevant regulations and standards relevant to your organization, including the AI, and ensure that your organization complies with all legal requirements.

- Advocate for Responsible AI: Engage with policymakers and industry groups to advocate for responsible AI practices and contribute to the development of AI governance frameworks.

Risk Management

- Identify Risks: Identify potential risks associated with AI development and deployment within your organization and develop strategies to mitigate these risks.
- Crisis Management: Prepare for potential crises by developing a crisis management plan. Ensure that your organization is trained to be able to effectively respond to unexpected challenges.

Continuous Learning and Adaptation

- Adapt to Change: Be prepared to adapt to changes, especially in the AI landscape, by staying flexible and open to new ideas and approaches.
- Continuous Improvement: Foster a culture of continuous improvement within your organization. Encourage your employees to seek out new learning opportunities and stay updated on industry trends.

Glossary of Key AI Terms

These definitions (which were all provided by Microsoft's CoPilot AI) are meant to provide you with a comprehensive overview of key AI terms, ensuring that, as an executive, you are well-equipped to understand and navigate the rapidly evolving AI landscape.

1. Adoption Rate: Measures the speed and extent to which new users or customers start using a product or service after its introduction, reflecting its acceptance and integration within a target audience.

2. Anonymization: The process of removing personally identifiable information (PII) from datasets, rendering individuals unidentifiable. This technique is crucial for protecting privacy while allowing organizations to analyze data for insights. Therefore, methods such as data masking, tokenization, and differential privacy can be employed to anonymize data effectively.

3. Artificial Intelligence (AI): The simulation of human intelligence in machines designed to perform tasks such as learning, reasoning, problem-solving, and decision-making. AI encompasses various subfields, including machine learning, natural language processing, and computer vision, and it has the potential to revolutionize numerous industries.

4. AI Agent: An autonomous software entity designed to perceive its environment, make decisions, and take actions to achieve specific goals or complete tasks.

5. AI Chatbots: These are AI systems designed to simulate human conversation, providing automated responses to user inquiries and facilitating interactive communication.

6. AI Winter: A period of reduced interest, funding, and research in AI. This usually occurs after high expectations for AI technology fail to materialize, leading to disillusionment among investors and researchers. The term draws from the idea of a "winter" being a cold and stagnant period.

7. Attribute-Based Access Control (ABAC): An authorization model that determines access rights based on attributes associated with users, resources, actions, and the environment.

8. Autonomous Vehicles: Self-driving vehicles that use AI to navigate, perceive the environment, and make decisions without human intervention. These vehicles rely on sensors, machine learning algorithms, and real-time data processing to operate safely and efficiently.

9. Benchmarking & Best Practices: In AI, they involve evaluating AI systems against industry standards and proven methodologies to ensure optimal performance, efficiency, and continuous improvement.

10. Bias: In AI, bias refers to systematic errors or prejudices that can lead to unfair or discriminatory outcomes. Bias often arises from biased training data or algorithms, and addressing it's essential for ensuring ethical AI that promotes fairness and equality.

11. Big Data: Extremely large datasets that require advanced analytical techniques and technologies to process, analyze, and extract valuable insights. Big data is characterized by its volume, velocity, variety, and veracity. Moreover, it plays a crucial role in training AI models.

12. Computer Vision: The field of AI that enables machines to interpret and understand visual information from the world, such as images and videos. Applications of computer vision include image recognition, object detection, facial recognition, and autonomous driving.

13. Convolution Neural Networks (CNNs): A type of deep learning model designed to automatically and adaptively learn spatial hierarchies of features from data.

14. Data Anonymization: It is the process of transforming personal data in such a way that it can no longer be traced back to individual entities, ensuring privacy and compliance with data protection regulations.

15. Data Annotation: This involves labeling data to provide context and meaning for AI algorithms.

16. Data Masking: The process of obscuring or anonymizing sensitive information within a dataset, allowing it to be used for testing, development, or analysis without exposing the actual data.

17. Data Silos: Isolated collections of data within an organization that are inaccessible to other departments, leading to inefficiencies and hindered decision-making.

18. Dataset Nutrition Labels: Standardized documentation tools that provide essential information about a dataset's contents, quality, and potential biases, helping users assess its suitability for specific use cases.

19. Decision Trees: Graphical representations used in machine learning and data analysis that split data into branches based on feature values (e.g., customer age, customer income, etc.), leading to a decision or prediction at each leaf node.

20. Deep Learning: A type of machine learning that uses neural networks with many layers (deep neural networks) to model complex patterns in data. Deep learning has achieved breakthroughs in areas such as image recognition, natural language processing, and autonomous systems, enabling machines to perform tasks with high accuracy.

21. Differential Privacy: A mathematical technique used to ensure individual privacy by adding controlled noise to data, allowing

for statistical analysis without having to reveal personal information.

22. Edge AI: The practice of running AI algorithms on devices at the edge of the network, close to where data is generated, to reduce latency and improve privacy. Edge AI is used in applications like autonomous vehicles, smart cities, and healthcare monitoring, where real-time data processing is critical.

23. Encryption: Transforms readable data into an unreadable format, making it accessible only to those with the decryption key.

24. Ethical AI: The practice of developing and deploying AI technologies in a manner that respects ethical principles, such as fairness, accountability, and transparency. Ethical AI aims to mitigate biases, ensure privacy, and promote responsible use of AI to benefit society.

25. Explainable AI (XAI): AI systems designed to provide clear and understandable explanations of their decisions and actions to users. XAI enhances transparency and trust by making AI's inner workings more comprehensible to humans, enabling better decision-making and accountability.

26. Facial Recognition: This is a biometric technology that identifies or verifies a person's identity by analyzing and comparing patterns based on their facial features.

27. Federated Learning: A distributed machine learning approach where multiple devices collaboratively train a model while

keeping the training data localized on each device. Federated learning enhances privacy by ensuring that sensitive data remains on the device and only model updates are shared.

28. Feedback Loops: In AI technology, it refers to the processes where the system's outputs are fed back as inputs to adjust and improve the system's performance over time, enabling continuous learning and optimization.

29. General AI (AGI): Refers to a type of AI that possesses the ability to understand, learn, and apply knowledge across a wide range of tasks and domains at a human-like level of competency.

30. Generative Adversarial Networks (GANs): A class of neural networks consisting of two models, a generator and a discriminator, that are trained together in a competitive setting. GANs can generate realistic synthetic data, such as images or text, by learning the underlying data distribution.

31. Generative AI: A type of AI that is capable of creating new content. This could include text, images, music, or even entire virtual environments. Unlike traditional AI systems, which are designed to recognize patterns and make decisions based on existing data, generative AI creates new data that is similar to the original training data.

32. Homomorphic Encryption: Allows computations on encrypted data without decrypting it, ensuring data privacy throughout the process.

33. Hyperparameter Tuning: The process of selecting the optimal hyperparameters for a machine learning model, such as learning rate, batch size, and the number of layers. Hyperparameter tuning is essential for improving the model's performance and achieving better results.

34. Human-Centric AI: Refers to AI systems designed with a primary focus on enhancing and improving human experiences, interactions, and well-being.

35. ImageNet: A large visual database designed for use in visual object recognition software research.

36. Incremental Development: In AI refers to the continuous and adaptive process of updating AI models with new data, allowing them to learn and improve over time without forgetting previously acquired knowledge.

37. Internet of Things (IoT): The network of physical objects embedded with sensors, software, and other technologies to connect and exchange data with other devices and systems over the Internet. IoT enables smart devices to communicate and interact in real time, facilitating applications such as smart homes, industrial automation, and environmental monitoring.

38. Intrapreneurial: The entrepreneurial mindset and activities undertaken by employees within an established organization.

39. Key Performance Indicators (KPIs): Measurable metrics used to evaluate the success and performance of an organization or specific initiatives.

40. Large Language Models (LLMs): A type of AI designed for natural language processing tasks. LLMs are trained on vast amounts of text data using self-supervised learning techniques, allowing them to understand and generate human-like text. Examples include OpenAI's GPT-3 and GPT-4, Google's LaMDA, and Hugging Face's BLOOM.

41. Local Interpretable Model-Agnostic Explanations (LIME): A technique designed to provide understandable and human-interpretable explanations of complex and black-box machine learning models at the individual prediction level.

42. Lisp Machines: Specialized computers in the 1980s optimized for AI research.

43. Machine Learning (ML): A subset of AI that enables machines to learn from data and improve their performance over time without being explicitly programmed. ML algorithms can identify patterns, make predictions, and optimize processes in various applications, such as recommendation systems, fraud detection, and autonomous driving.

44. Model Cards: Detailed documentation tools that provide essential information about machine learning, including their performance, limitations, and intended use cases.

45. Model Training: In AI, it involves feeding data to an algorithm to enable it to learn patterns and make predictions or decisions based on that data.

46. Multi-Party Computation: Where multiple parties can jointly compute a function over their inputs while keeping those inputs private.

47. Narrow AI (ANI): Refers to AI systems that are designed and trained to perform a specific task or a limited set of tasks, such as language translation or facial recognition, and cannot perform tasks outside of their predefined capabilities.

48. Natural Language Generation (NLG): A subfield of NLP focused on generating coherent and contextually relevant natural language text from structured data or other forms of input. NLG is used in applications like automated report writing, chatbots, and content creation.

49. Natural Language Processing (NLP): The branch of AI that focuses on the interaction between computers and human language, enabling machines to understand, interpret, and generate human language. NLP applications include chatbots, language translation, sentiment analysis, and text summarization.

50. Neural Networks: Computational models inspired by the human brain, consisting of interconnected nodes (neurons) that process information in layers. Neural networks are the foundation of

deep learning and are used in tasks like image recognition, language processing, and game playing.

51. Parallel Processing: A method of simultaneously breaking down and processing multiple tasks across various processors to achieve faster computation[cccl], with there being two primary types such as data parallelism and task parallelism.

52. Predictive Maintenance: The use of AI and data analytics to predict when equipment or machinery is likely to fail, allowing for proactive maintenance to avoid downtime and reduce costs. Predictive maintenance relies on real-time monitoring, historical data analysis, and machine learning algorithms.

53. Process Mining Tools: Software applications designed to analyze and improve business processes by extracting knowledge from event logs recorded by an organization's information systems.

54. Prompt Engineering: The practice of crafting precise and effective input prompts to guide AI models in producing accurate, relevant, and desired outputs.

55. Quantum Computing: A type of computing that leverages quantum mechanics to perform calculations at speeds significantly faster than traditional computers. Quantum computing has potential applications in AI, cryptography, complex simulations, and optimization problems.

56. Recommendation Systems: AI-driven tools that analyze user preferences and behaviors to suggest relevant items or content, such as movies, products, or articles.

57. Recurrent Neural Networks (RNNs): A type of neural network designed to handle sequential data by utilizing feedback loops, allowing them to maintain a memory of previous inputs and capture temporal dependencies.

58. Reinforcement Learning: A type of machine learning where an agent learns to make decisions by interacting with an environment and receiving rewards or penalties based on its actions. The agent aims to maximize its cumulative reward over time by learning the optimal policy.

59. Reskilling: Refers to the process of teaching employees new skills to perform a different job or adapt to a new role within the organization.

60. Robotic Process Automation (RPA): The use of software robots (or "bots") to automate repetitive and rule-based tasks traditionally performed by humans, enhancing efficiency and reducing error rates in business processes.

61. Role-Based Access Control (RBAC): A method of regulating access to computer systems and data based on the roles assigned to individual users within an organization.

62. Shapley Additive Explanations (SHAP): A method used in machine learning to fairly distribute the contribution of each

feature to the overall prediction, providing interpretable insights into the model's decisions.

63. Small Language Models (SMLs): Compact AI systems designed to efficiently process, understand, and generate natural language, often tailored for specific tasks or resource-constrained environments.

64. Smart Cities: Urban areas that leverage AI and IoT technologies to optimize infrastructure, enhance public services, and improve resident's quality of life. Smart city applications include traffic management, energy efficiency, public safety, and environmental monitoring.

65. Speech Recognition: The technology that enables machines to convert spoken language into text. Speech recognition systems use machine learning models to analyze audio signals and recognize words, facilitating applications like voice assistants and transcription services.

66. Superintelligent AI: Refers to an AI system that surpasses human intelligence and capabilities across virtually all aspects of cognition, including problem-solving, learning, and creativity.

67. Supervised Learning: A type of machine learning where the model is trained on labeled data, meaning the input data is paired with the correct output. The model learns to map inputs to outputs based on this training data, allowing it to make predictions on new and unseen data.

68. Synthetic AI Data: Artificially generated datasets created using algorithms or simulations, often to augment real-world data for training, testing, or enhancing machine learning models.

69. Tensor Processing Units (TPUs): Custom-designed to accelerate machine learning workloads, providing significant performance improvements over traditional CPUs and GPUs for specific AI tasks.

70. Tokenization: The process of converting sensitive data into non-sensitive equivalents called tokens, which can be used in place of the original data without compromising its security.

71. Transfer Learning: A machine learning technique where a pre-trained model on one task is fine-tuned on a different but related task. Transfer learning leverages knowledge gained from the initial task to improve performance on the new task with less training data.

72. Upskilling: Refers to the process of teaching employees new skills and competencies to enhance their performance and adapt to evolving job requirements.

73. Unsupervised Learning: A type of machine learning where the model is trained on unlabeled data, meaning the input data does not have corresponding output labels. The model identifies patterns and structures in the data, such as clustering similar data points or reducing dimensionality.

74. Usage Frequency: Measures how often users engage with a product or service within a given period, reflecting its relevance and value to them.

75. User Engagement: The measure of how actively and consistently users interact with a product, service, or content, reflecting their interest, satisfaction, and overall experience.

76. Variational Autoencoder (VAE): A type of generative model in machine learning that is used for unsupervised learning and data generation.

77. Virtual Assistants: AI-powered software applications designed to perform tasks or services for individuals, such as scheduling appointments, answering questions, or managing smart home devices through natural language interactions.

[i] No Author Stated, (No Date Stated), "Talos" published at greekmythology.com.
[ii] Coursera Staff, (No Date Stated but Updated in 2024), "The History of AI: A Timeline of Artificial Intelligence" published at coursera.org.
[iii] Russell, S., & Norvig, P., (2021), *Artificial Intelligence: A Modern Approach (4th Edition),* Pearson.
[iv] Coursera Staff, (No Date Stated but Updated in 2024), "The History of AI: A Timeline of Artificial Intelligence" published at coursera.org.
[v] Turing, A. M., (1950), "Computing Machinery and Intelligence," *Mind*, Vol. 49(236), and published at courses.cs.umbc.edu.
[vi] Hodges, A., (2014), *Alan Turing: The Enigma*, Princeton University Press.
[vii] McCarthy, J., Minsky, M., Rochester, N., & Shannon, C., (Drafted in 1956), "A Proposal for the Dartmouth Summer Research Project on Artificial Intelligence" and published in *AI Magazine* in 2006 and at ojs.aaai.org.
[viii] Newell, A., & Simon, H. A., (1956), "The Logic Theory Machine--A Complex Information Processing System" published by Rand Corporation at rand.org.
[ix] Glover, E. & Updated by Whitfield, B., (No Date Stated but Updated 2023), "What is AI Winter?" published at builtin.com.
[x] Rosenblatt, F., (1958), "The perceptron: A probabilistic model for information storage and organization in the brain," *Psychological Review*, 65(6), 386-408; Crevier, D., (1993), *AI: The Tumultuous History of the Search for Artificial Intelligence*, Basic Books.
[xi] Ivakhnenko, A. G., (1968), "Group Method of Data Handling-A Rival Method of Stochastic Approximation," *Soviet Automatic Control,* 1(3), 43-55.
[xii] Hinton, G. E., Rumelhart, D. E., & Williams, R. J., (1986), "Learning representations by back-propagating errors," *Nature*, Vol. 323, Issue 6088, 533-536; Foote, K. D., (2022), "A Brief History of Deep Learning" published at dataversity.net.
[xiii] *Krizhevsky, A., Sutskever, I., & Hinton, G. E., (2012),* "ImageNet classification with deep convolutional neural networks," presented at NeurIPS 2012, and published at paperswithcode.com.
[xiv] No Author Stated, (No Date Stated but Updated in 2025), "ImageNet" published by en.m.wikipedia.org.
[xv] Chetlur, S., Woolley, C., Vandermersch, P., Cohen, J., Tran, J., Catanzaro, B., & Shelhamer, E., (2014). "cuDNN: Efficient Primitives for Deep Learning," published on *arXiv preprint arXiv*:1410.0759, and at arxiv.org.

xvi No Author Stated, (No Date Stated but Updated in 2025), "Processing? Definition, Types, and Examples" published at spiceworks.com.

xvii Chakraborty, A., (No Date Stated but Updated in 2019), "Data parallelism vs Task parallelism" published at tutorialspoint.com.

xviii Agarwal, T., (2013), "Introducing NVIDIA's Compute Unified Device Architecture (CUDA)" published at pages.cs.wisc.edu.

xix Jouppi, N. P., Young, C., Patil, N., Patterson, D., Agrawal, G., Bajwa, R., ... & Clary, A., (2017), "In-datacenter performance analysis of a tensor processing unit," In 2017 ACM/IEEE 44th Annual International Symposium on Computer Architecture (ISCA), and published at arxiv.org.

xx Condon, S., (2017), "Intel unveils the Nervana Neural Network Processor" published at zdnet.com; AMD, (2016), "AMD introduces Radeon Instinct: Accelerating Machine Intelligence" published at amd.com.

xxi Abadi, M., Barham, P., Chen, J., Chen, Z., Davis, A., Dean, J., ... & Zheng, X., (2016), "TensorFlow: A system for large-scale machine learning," In 12th (USENIX) Symposium on Operating Systems Design and Implementation ((OSDI) 16) published at arxiv.org; Paszke, A., Gross, S., Massa, F., Lerer, A., Bradbury, J., Chanan, G., ... & Chintala, S., (2019), "PyTorch: An imperative style, high-performance deep learning library," arXiv preprint arXiv:1912.01703, and published at arxiv.org.

xxii Chollet, F., (2015), "Keras: The Python Deep Learning library" published at github.com.

xxiii Nag, D., (2025), "The Interplay Between AI Software and Hardware" published at sitepronews.com.

xxiv Crevier, D., (1993), *AI: The Tumultuous History of the Search for Artificial Intelligence*. Basic Books.

xxv Dreyfus, H. L., (1972), *What Computers Can't Do: A Critique of Artificial Reason*, Harper & Row.

xxvi Lighthill, J., (1973), "Artificial Intelligence: A General Survey," In Artificial Intelligence: a paper symposium commissioned by the Science Research Council (SRC), and published at rodsmith.nz.

xxvii McCorduck, P., (2004), *Machines Who Think: A Personal Inquiry into the History and Prospects of Artificial Intelligence*. A. K. Peters, Ltd.

xxviii Crevier, D., (1993), *AI: The Tumultuous History of the Search for Artificial Intelligence*, Basic Books.

xxix Nilsson, N. J., (2009), *The Quest for Artificial Intelligence*, Cambridge University Press.

xxx Russell, S., & Norvig, P., (2021), *Artificial Intelligence: A Modern Approach (4th Edition)*, Pearson.

[xxxi] Campbell, M., Hoane, A. J., & Hsu, F. H., (2002), "Deep Blue," *Artificial Intelligence*, 134(1-2), and published at core.ac.uk.

[xxxii] LeCun, Y., Bengio, Y., & Hinton, G., (2015), "Deep learning," *Nature*, 521(7553), and published at hal.science/hal-04206682/file/Lecun2015.pdf.

[xxxiii] *Krizhevsky, A., Sutskever, I., & Hinton, G. E., (2012),* "ImageNet classification with deep convolutional neural networks," presented at NeurlPS 2012, and published at paperswithcode.com.

[xxxiv] Abadi, M., Barham, P., Chen, J., Chen, Z., Davis, A., Dean, J., ... & Zheng, X., (2016), "TensorFlow: A system for large-scale machine learning," In 12th (USENIX) Symposium on Operating Systems Design and Implementation ((OSDI) 16) published at arxiv.org; Paszke, A., Gross, S., Massa, F., Lerer, A., Bradbury, J., Chanan, G., ... & Chintala, S., (2019), "PyTorch: An imperative style, high-performance deep learning library," arXiv preprint arXiv:1912.01703, and published at arxiv.org.

[xxxv] Silver, D., Huang, A., Maddison, C. J., Guez, A., Sifre, L., van den Driessche, G., ... & Hassabis, D., (2016), "Mastering the game of Go with deep neural networks and tree search," *Nature*, 529(7587), and published at nature.com.

[xxxvi] Goodfellow, I., Bengio, Y., & Courville, A., (2016), *Deep Learning*, MIT Press.

[xxxvii] Goodfellow, I., Bengio, Y., & Courville, A., (2016), *Deep Learning*, MIT Press.

[xxxviii] Hastie, T., Tibshirani, R., & Friedman, J., (2009), *The Elements of Statistical Learning: Data Mining, Inference, and Prediction.* Springer, Vol. 2.

[xxxix] LeCun, Y., Bengio, Y., & Hinton, G., (2015), "Deep learning," *Nature*, 521(7553) published and at hal.science/hal-04206682/file/Lecun2015.pdf; Zhao, X., Wang, L., Zhang, Y., Han, X., Deveci, M., & Parmar, M., (2024), "A review of convolutional neural networks in computer vision" published by *Artificial Intelligence Review*, 57(99), and at link.springer.com; Mienye, I., Swart, T., & Obaido, G., (2024), "Recurrent Neural Networks: A Comprehensive Review of Architectures, Variants and Applications" published by *Information*, 15(9), and at mdpi.com.

[xl] Bertsimasa, D., & Li, M., (2020), "Scalable Holistic Linear Regression," published by Operations Research Letters - MIT and at dspace.mit.edu; Torres, A., & Akbaritabar, A., (2024), "The use of linear models in quantitative research," published by *Quantitative Science Studies*, 5(2), and at direct.mit.edu; Mahendran, A., Thompson, H., & McGree, J., (2023), "A model robust subsampling approach for Generalised Linear Models in big data settings," published by *Statistical Papers*, 64, and at link.springer.com.

[xli] Jurafsky, D., & Martin, J. H. (2009), *Speech and Language Processing (2nd Edition)*, Pearson, Vol. 2.

[xlii] Szeliski, R., (2010*)*, *Computer Vision: Algorithms and Applications*, Springer.

[xliii] Sutton, R. S., & Barto, A. G., (2018), *Reinforcement Learning: An Introduction (2nd Edition),* MIT Press.

[xliv] O'Neil, C., *Weapons of Math Destruction: How Big Data Increases Inequality and Threatens Democracy*. Crown, 2016.

[xlv] Russell, S., & Norvig, P., (2021), *Artificial Intelligence: A Modern Approach (4th Edition),* Pearson.

[xlvi] Goodfellow, I., Bengio, Y., & Courville, A., (2016), *Deep Learning*, MIT Press.

[xlvii] Szeliski, R., (2011), *Computer Vision: Algorithms and Applications,* Springer.

[xlviii] Bostrom, N., (2014), *Superintelligence: Paths, Dangers, Strategies*, published by Oxford University Press and at ia800501.us.archive.org/5/items/superintelligence-paths-dangers-srategies-by-nick-bostrom/superintelligence-paths-dangers-strategies-by-nick-bostrom.pdf.

[xlix] Bostrom, N., (2014), *Superintelligence: Paths, Dangers, Strategies*, published by Oxford University Press and at ia800501.us.archive.org/5/items/superintelligence-paths-dangers-srategies-by-nick-bostrom/superintelligence-paths-dangers-strategies-by-nick-bostrom.pdf.

[l] Provost, F., & Fawcett, T., (2013), *Data Science for Business: What You Need to Know about Data Mining and Data-Analytic Thinking*, O'Reilly Media.

[li] Han, J., Pei, J., & Kamber, M. (2012). *Data Mining: Concepts and Techniques (3rd Edition),* published by Morgan Kaufmann.

[lii] Goodfellow, I., Bengio, Y., & Courville, A., (2016), *Deep Learning*, MIT Press.

[liii] Mayer-Schönberger, V., & Cukier, K., (2013), *Big Data: A Revolution That Will Transform How We Live, Work, and Think*, Harper Business.

[liv] Zarsky, T. Z., (2017), "Incompatible: The GDPR in the Age of Big Data," *Seton Hall Law Review*, Vol. 47, and published at papers.ssrn.com.

[lv] Jurafsky, D., & Martin, J. H., (2009), *Speech and Language Processing (2nd Edition),* Pearson, Vol. 2.

[lvi] Cairo, M., (2023), "Synthetic Data and GDPR Compliance: How Artificial Intelligence Might Resolve the Privacy-Utility Tradeoff," published by the *Journal of Technology Law & Policy: A law journal publication of the University of Florida Levin College of Law,* Volume 28, and at journaloftechlaw.org.

[lvii] Sutton, R. S., & Barto, A. G., (2018), *Reinforcement Learning: An Introduction (2nd Edition),* MIT Press.

[lviii] Topol, E. J., (2019), *Deep Medicine: How Artificial Intelligence Can Make Healthcare Human Again*, Basic Books.

[lix] Jha, S., & Topol, E. J., (2016), "Adapting to Artificial Intelligence: Radiologists and Pathologists as Information Specialists," *JAMA*, 316(22), and published at jamanetwork.com.

[lx] Collins, F. S., & Varmus, H., (2015), "A new initiative on precision medicine," *New England Journal of Medicine*, 372(9), and published at nejm.org.

[lxi] Keyl, J., Keyl, P., Klauschen, F., & Kleesiek, J., (2025), "Artificial Intelligence improves personalized cancer treatment," *Nature Center*, (5)(1), and published at lmu.de.

[lxii] Jiang, F., Jiang, Y., Zhi, H., Dong, Y., Li, H., Ma, S., ... & Wang, Y., (2017), "Artificial intelligence in healthcare: past, present and future," *Stroke and Vascular Neurology*, 2017;0: e000101. doi:10.1136/svn-2017-000101, and published at svn.bmj.com.

[lxiii] Wang, Y., Kung, L. A., & Byrd, T. A., (2018), "Big data analytics: Understanding its capabilities and potential benefits for healthcare organizations," *Technological Forecasting and Social Change*, 126, and published at ehidc.org.

[lxiv] Aggarwal, C. C., (2015), *Outlier Analysis*, Springer.

[lxv] Chan, E. P., (2017), *Algorithmic Trading: Winning Strategies and Their Rationale*, Wiley.

[lxvi] Westerman, G., Bonnet, D., & McAfee, A., (2014), *Leading Digital: Turning Technology into Business Transformation*, Harvard Business Press.

[lxvii] Davenport, T. H., Guha, A., Grewal, D., & Bressgott, T., (2020), "How artificial intelligence will change the future of marketing," *Journal of the Academy of Marketing Science*, 48(1), published at ide.mit.edu.

[lxviii] Smith, C., & Linden, G., (2017), "Two decades of recommender systems at Amazon.com," *IEEE Internet Computing*, 21(3), and published at amazon.science/publications/two-decades-of-recommender-systems-at-amazon-com.

[lxix] Fildes, R., Ma, S., & Kolassa, S., (2022), "Retail forecasting: Research and practice," *International Journal of Forecasting*, 38(4), and published at eprints.lancs.ac.uk.

[lxx] Hübner, A., Kuhn, H., & Sternbeck, M. G., (2013), "Demand and supply chain planning in grocery retail: an operations planning framework,"

International Journal of Retail & Distribution Management, 41(7), and published at emerald.com.

[lxxi] Christopher, M., (2016), *Logistics & Supply Chain Management*, Pearson UK.

[lxxii] Ivanov, D., & Das, A., (2020), "Coronavirus (COVID-19/SARS-CoV-2) and supply chain resilience: a research note," *International Journal of Integrated Supply Management*, 13(1), and published at researchgate.net.

[lxxiii] Jardine, A. K. S., Lin, D., & Banjevic, D., (2006), "A review on machinery diagnostics and prognostics implementing condition-based maintenance," *Mechanical Systems and Signal Processing*, 20(7), published at daneshyari.com.

[lxxiv] Mobley, R. K., (2002), *An Introduction to Predictive Maintenance*, Butterworth-Heinemann.

[lxxv] No Author Stated, (2025), "How to Use AI for Quality Control" published at saiwa.ai.

[lxxvi] Raghuwanshi, P., (2024), "Revolutionizing Semiconductor Design and Manufacturing with AI," *Journal of Knowledge Learning and Science Technology*, 3(3), and published at researchgate.net.

[lxxvii] Groover, M. P., (2018), *Automation, Production Systems, and Computer-Integrated Manufacturing*, Pearson.

[lxxviii] Buchanan, J. T., (2019), *Robotic Process Automation: A Guide for Decision Makers*, Springer.

[lxxix] Cubiss, J., (2025), "How AI Is Changing The Game In Manufacturing" published at forbes.com; No Author Stated, (No Date Stated), "Predictive maintenance and smart factor" published at www2.deloitte.com.

[lxxx] Cubiss, J., (2025), "How AI Is Changing The Game In Manufacturing" published at forbes.com; No Author Stated, (No Date Stated), "Predictive maintenance and smart factor" published at www2.deloitte.com.

[lxxxi] Litman, T., (2021), "Autonomous Vehicle Implementation Predictions: Implications for Transport Planning" published by Victoria Transport Policy Institute at vtpi.org.

[lxxxii] Levinson, D., (2011), *The Transportation Experience: Policy, Planning, and Deployment (3rd Edition)*, Oxford University Press.

[lxxxiii] Company News, The Waymo & Swiss RE Teams, (2023), "Waymo's autonomous vehicles are significantly safter than human-driven ones, says new research led by Swiss Re" published at waymo.com.

[lxxxiv] Gordon, P., & Wong, H., (2019), *Managing Urban Traffic: Insights and Case Studies*, Wiley, (Vol. 2).

[lxxxv] Schrank, D., Eisele, B., & Lomax, T., (2019), "2019 Urban Mobility Report," published by the Texas A&M Transportation Institute at static.tti.tamu.edu.

[lxxxvi] Christopher, M., (2016), *Logistics & Supply Chain Management (5th Edition)*, Pearon UK.

[lxxxvii] Rushton, A., Croucher, P., & Baker, P., (2017), *The Handbook of Logistics and Distribution Management: Understanding the Supply Chain (5th Edition)*, Kogan Page.

[lxxxviii] McKinnon, A., Browne, M., Whiteing, A., & Piecyk, M., (2015), *Green Logistics: Improving the Environmental Sustainability of Logistics*, Kogan Page, (Vol. 4).

[lxxxix] Chaffey, D., & Ellis-Chadwick, F., (2019), *Digital Marketing: Strategy, Implementation and Practice (7th Edition)*, Pearson.

[xc] Davenport, T. H., & Ronanki, R., (2018), "Artificial Intelligence for the Real World," published by *Harvard Business Review* at hbr.org.

[xci] Kotler, P., Kartajaya, H., & Setiawan, I., (2021), *Marketing 5.0: Technology for Humanity*, Wiley.

[xcii] Rust, R. T., & Huang, M. H., (2014), "The Service Revolution and the Transformation of Marketing," *Journal of Marketing*, 33(3), and published at econpapers.repec.org.

[xciii] Fisher, C. D., & Schoenfeldt, L. F., (2017), *Human Resource Management (9th Edition)*, Houghton Mifflin.

[xciv] Stone, D. L., Deadrick, D. L., Lukaszewski, K. M., & Johnson, R., (2020), "The Influence of Technology on the Future of Human Resource Management," *Human Resource Management Review* at psycnet.apa.org.

[xcv] Corn, M., (2024), "Best AI-Driven Employee Engagement Tools in 2025" published at challengingvoice.com.

[xcvi] Bassi, L., & McMurrer, D., (2007), "Maximizing Your Return on People," published by *Harvard Business Review* at hbr.org.

[xcvii] Topol, E., (2019), *Deep Medicine: How Artificial Intelligence Can Make Healthcare Human Again*, Basic Books.

[xcviii] Obermeyer, Z., & Emanuel, E. J., (2016), "Predicting the Future — Big Data, Machine Learning, and Clinical Medicine," *New England Journal of Medicine*, 375(13), and published at scholar.harvard.edu.

[xcix] No Author Stated, (2024), "AI-Powered Fraud Detection In Banking: Strengthening Financial Security" published at sapidblue.com.

[c] Nigrini, M. J., (2013), *Forensic Analytics: Methods and Techniques for Forensic Accounting Investigations*, Wiley.

ci Bessis, J., (2019), *Risk Management in Banking*, Wiley, (Vol. 4).

cii Davenport, T. H., & Ronanki, R., (2018), "Artificial Intelligence for the Real World" published at *Havard Business Review* at hbr.org; Hoenig; H, (No Date Stated but Updated in 2025), "Understanding Market Segmentation; A Comprehensive Guide" published at investopedia.com.

ciii Russell, S., & Norvig, P., (2021), *Artificial Intelligence: A Modern Approach (4th Edition),* Pearson.

civ Agrawal, A., Gans, J. S., & Goldfarb, A., (2022), *Prediction Machines, Updated and Expanded: The Simple Economics of Artificial Intelligence* Harvard Business Publishing at hbsp.harvard.edu.

cv Rüssmann, M., Lorenz, M., Gerbert, P., Waldner, M., Justus, J., Engel, P., & Harnisch, M., (2015), "Industry 4.0: The Future of Productivity and Growth in Manufacturing Industries," published at bdg.com.

cvi Lee, J., Kao, H. A., & Yang, S., (2014), "Service Innovation and Smart Analytics for Industry 4.0 and Big Data Environment" published at euro.ecom.cmu.edu.

cvii Prince Sharma, (2024), "How did General Motors Implemented IBM Watson for Predictive Maintenance?" published at orgevo.in.

cviii Chavan, R.D., & Sambare, G.B., (2024), "AI-Driven Traffic Management Systems in Smart Cities: A Review," *Educational Administration: Theory and Practice*, 30(5), and published at kuey.net.

cix Papageorgiou, M., Diakaki, C., Dinopoulou, V., Kotsialos, A., & Wang, Y., (2003), "Review of Road Traffic Control Strategies" published by IEEE at ieeexplore.ieee.org.

cx Smith, S., Barlow, G., Xie, X.-F., & Rubenstein, Z., (2013), "SURTRAC: Scalable Urban Traffic Control," Carnegie Mellon University published at ri.cmu.edu.

cxi Chaffey, D., & Ellis-Chadwick, F., (2019), *Digital Marketing: Strategy, Implementation and Practice (7th Edition),* Pearson.

cxii Kotler, P., Kartajaya, H., & Setiawan, I., (2021), *Marketing 5.0: Technology for Humanity,* Wiley.

cxiii Stone, D. L., Deadrick, D. L., Lukaszewski, K. M., & Johnson, R., (2020), "The Influence of Technology on the Future of Human Resource Management," *Human Resource Management Review*, 25(2), published at psycnet.apa.org.

cxiv Fisher, C. D., & Schoenfeldt, L. F., (2017), *Human Resource Management (9th Edition),* Houghton Mifflin.

cxv No Author Stated, (No Date Stated), "AI-powered employee retention: using data to reduce turnover" published at quinyx.com; Vorecol Editorial Team,

(2024), "How can AI and data analytics enhance employee experience management strategies?" published at vorecol.com.

[cxvi] Provost, F., & Fawcett, T., (2013), *Data Science for Business: What You Need to Know about Data Mining and Data-Analytic Thinking*, O'Reilly Media.

[cxvii] Hastie, T., Tibshirani, R., & Friedman, J., (2009), *The Elements of Statistical Learning: Data Mining, Inference, and Prediction.* Springer, Vol. 2.

[cxviii] Goodfellow, I., Bengio, Y., & Courville, A., (2016), *Deep Learning*, MIT Press.

[cxix] Russell, S., & Norvig, P., (2021), *Artificial Intelligence: A Modern Approach (4th Edition)*, Pearson.

[cxx] Sutton, R. S., & Barto, A. G., (2018*), Reinforcement Learning: An Introduction (2nd Edition)*, MIT Press.

[cxxi] Bostrom, N., (2014), *Superintelligence: Paths, Dangers, Strategies*, published by Oxford University Press and at ia800501.us.archive.org/5/items/superintelligence-paths-dangers-srategies-by-nick-bostrom/superintelligence-paths-dangers-strategies-by-nick-bostrom.pdf.

[cxxii] Goodfellow, I., Bengio, Y., & Courville, A., (2016), *Deep Learning*, MIT Press.

[cxxiii] Porter, M. E., (1980), *Competitive Strategy: Techniques for Analyzing Industries and Competitors*, The Free Press.

[cxxiv] Aarfi, S., & Ahmed, N., (2024), "Prompt Engineering for Generative AI: Practical Techniques and Applications" published by *Software Engineering 2024,* 11(2), and at researchgate.net.

[cxxv] Eliot, L., (2024), "The Best Prompt Engineering Techniques For Getting The Most Out Of Generative AI" published at forbes.com.

[cxxvi] Valliani, J., (2024), "The ultimate guide to writing effective AI prompts" published at atlassian.com.

[cxxvii] No Author Stated, (2025), "What is Context in Prompt Engineering? Here's Everything You Need To Know" published at godofprompt.ai.

[cxxviii] No Author Stated, (2024), "Why Specifying Format in Prompt Engineering is Crucial" published at collegenp.com.

[cxxix] Ramlochan, S., (2024), "Intention-Aligned Prompting in AI Interactions" published at promptengineering.org.

[cxxx] Winter, T., (2024), "Tone of Voice Examples [With AI prompts & Content Sample]" published at seowind.io.

[cxxxi] Miguelañez, C., (2025), "Iterative Prompt Refinement: Step-by-Step Guide" published at latitude-blog.ghost.io.

[cxxxii] Sharma, S., (2024), "Guiding Tone and Style through Prompts: Influencing the AI Writing Style" published at surajsharma.net.

[cxxxiii] No Author Stated, (2025), "How ChatGPT Adapts to Different Writing Styles and Tones" published at theaipromptshop.com.

[cxxxiv] Rojo-Echeburúa, A., (2024), "Zero-Shot Prompting: Examples, Theory, Use Cases" published at datacamp.com.

[cxxxv] Rojo-Echeburúa, A., (2024), "Few-Shot Prompting: Examples, Theories ,Use Cases" published at datacamp.com.

[cxxxvi] No Author Stated, (No Date Stated), "Break Down Your Prompts for Better AI Results" published at relevanceai.com.

[cxxxvii] Mitrovic, S., (2024), "Prompts for Ethical AI Development: Guidelines and Examples" published at promptsty.com.

[cxxxviii] No Author Stated, (No Date Stated), "When AI Gets It Wrong: Addressing AI Hallucinations and Bias" published at mitsloanedtech.mit.edu.

[cxxxix] Schuster, D., Benevento, E., Aloini, D., & van der Aalst, W.M.P., (2024), "Analyzing Healthcare Processes with Incremental Process Discovery: Practical Insights from a Real-World Application" published by *Journal of Healthcare Informatics Research*, 8, and at link.springer.com; Henshall, A., (2018), "What is Process Mining? 9 Tools to Optimize Your Process Management" published at process.st.

[cxl] Ajeet, (2024), "AI in Customer Service: 10 Use Cases of AI-Powered RPA" published at ahex.co.

[cxli] Bain, W., (2024), "Transforming Real-Time Analytics with AI-Powered Digital Twins" published at dataversity.net.

[cxlii] Nieto-Rodriguez, A., & Vargas, R.V., (2023), "How AI Will Transform Project Management" published by *Harvard Business Review* at hbr.org.

[cxliii] Bednarski, D., (2025), "14 Best AI Collaboration Tools for Remote Teams" published at taskade.com.

[cxliv] Pudi, M., (2025), "Driving Retail Transformation with AI-Powered Customer Analytics" published at techbullion.com.

[cxlv] Raza, I., (2025), "Predictive Analytics in Healthcare" published at data.folio3.com.

[cxlvi] Hird, T., (2025), "How AI-Enabled Finance Functions Can Help Companies Navigate Macroeconomic Challenges More Effectively" published by Robert Half at roberthalf.com.

[cxlvii] Khneyzer, C., Boustany, Z., & Dagher, J., (2024), "AI-Driven Chatbots in CRM: Economic and Managerial Implications across Industries" published by *Administrative Science Journal* and at researchgate.net; Kulpa, J., (2017), "Why is Customer Relationship Management So Important?" published at forbes.com.

[cxlviii] Mercier, V., (2024), "AI in Hospitality: Creating Personalized Customer Experience" published at hotelnewsresource.com.

[cxlix] Candiani, S., (2024), "Transforming Telecoms with AI" published at microsoft.com.

[cl] Viliavin, R., (2023), "Customer Support: Using AI Chatbots for Efficiency and Empathy" published at forbes.com.

[cli] No Author Stated, (No Date Stated), "Speed Up Resolution Times with AI: The Answer to Faster Customer Service" published at sundevs.com.

[clii] Webio, (No Date Stated), "How do AI Agents Improve Efficiency in High-Volume Customer Engagement?" published at webio.com.

[cliii] Wizr AI, (2024), "Building Intelligent Systems: Leveraging Generative AI for Customer Sentiment Analysis" published at wizr.ai.

[cliv] Steinle, S., & Saueressig, T., (2025), "Transforming Customer Support with Artificial Intelligence" published at news.sap.com.

[clv] Murf, (2024), "AI Translation in Customer Support: Benefits and Challenges" published at murf.ai.

[clvi] TyCoonstory, (2024), "AI-Powered Translation: Enhancing Accuracy in Customer Support" published at tycoonstory.com.

[clvii] Kotler, P., Kartajaya, H., & Setiawan, I, (2016), *Marketing 4.0: Moving from Traditional to Digital*, Wiley.

[clviii] Artun, O., & Levin, D., (2015), *Predictive Marketing: Easy Ways Every Marketer Can Use Customer Analytics and Big Data*, Wiley.

[clix] Paczkowski, W., (2018), *Pricing Analytics: Models and Advanced Quantitative Techniques for Product Pricing,* Routledge.

[clx] Quadros, M., (No Date Stated), "The Role of AI in Personalizing the eCommerce Experience" published at blog.shift4shop.com.

[clxi] Ingram, T., LaForge, R., Avila, R., Schwepker, Jr., C., & Williams, M., (2019), *Sales Management: Analysis and Decision Making (10th Edition)*, Routledge.

[clxii] Jordan, J., & Vazzana, M., (2011), *Cracking the Sales Management Code: The Secrets to Measuring and Managing Sales Performance*, McGraw-Hill Education.

[clxiii] Goodman, J., (2014), *Customer Experience 3.0: High-Profit Strategies in the Age of Techno Service*, AMACOM.

[clxiv] Siegel, E., (2013), *Predictive Analytics: The Power to Predict Who Will Click, Buy, Lie, or Die*, Wiley.

[clxv] Paczkowski, W., (2018), *Pricing Analytics: Models and Advanced Quantitative Techniques for Product Pricing,* Routledge.

[clxvi] Siegel, E., (2013), *Predictive Analytics: The Power to Predict Who Will Click, Buy, Lie, or Die*, Wiley.

clxvii Paczkowski, W., (2018), *Pricing Analytics: Models and Advanced Quantitative Techniques for Product Pricing,* Routledge.

clxviii No Author Stated, (No Date Stated), "Optimise 5 Areas with AI Pricing and Analytics to Stay Ahead in the Future" published at symson.com.

clxix No Author Stated, (No Date Stated), "Optimise 5 Areas with AI Pricing and Analytics to Stay Ahead in the Future" published at symson.com.

clxx No Author Stated but Edited by Rana, N., Slade, E., Ganesh, S., Kizgin, H., Singh, N., Dey, B., Gutierrez, A., & Dwivedi, Y., (2020), *Digital and Social Media Marketing: Emerging Applications and Theoretical Development*, edited by Durgesh K. Srivastava and Avinash Kapoor, Routledge.

clxxi Hilpisch, Y., (2020), *Artificial Intelligence in Finance*, O'Reilly Media.

clxxii No Author Stated, (No Date Stated), "The Role of Artificial Intelligence in Fraud Detection and Prevention" published at kiya.ai.

clxxiii No Author Stated, (No Date Stated), "The Impact of AI on Scaling Personalized Guest Experiences" published at socialhospitality.com.

clxxiv Michalis, B., (2024), "Check-in Redefined: Unleash the Power of Automated Hotel Check-In" published at canarytechnologies.com.

clxxv IT Medical, (2024), "Transforming Patient Care: The Role of AI-Powered Assistants" published at medcitynews.com.

clxxvi Topol, E., (2019), *Deep Medicine: How Artificial Intelligence Can Make Healthcare Human Again*, Basic Books.

clxxvii Cosmas, A., & Krishnan, V., (2023), "What AI means for travel - now and in the future" published at mckinsey.com.

clxxviii Heber, C., (2023), "The Role Of Chatbots In The Future Of The Travel Industry" published at forbes.com.

clxxix Miller, V., (2025), "Enhancing Telecom Networks with AI-Driven Predictive Maintenance" published at techbullion.com.

clxxx Kaur Gill, J., (2024), "Reimagining Personalized Plan Recommendations with AI Agents" published at akira.ai.

clxxxi Anderson, J., (2024), "Your AI Readiness Assessment Checklist" published at icma.org.

clxxxii Merzlova, K., (2025), "Integrating AI into Business: A Complete Guide for 2025" published at sumatosoft.com.

clxxxiii Etlinger, S., (2024), "The AI Strategy Roadmap: Navigating the stages of value creation," published by The Microsoft Cloud at Microsoft.com.

clxxxiv Keerthan, S.J., (No Date Stated by Updated in 2025), "30+ Best AI Tools For Businesses" published at thinkstack.ai.

clxxxv Shivanna, A., (2024), "Building A Data Strategy For Successful AI Implementation" published at forbes.com.

clxxxvi Wrenn, K., & Sohn, E., (2021), "Navigating AI Change Management Like a Boss" published at boozallen.com.

clxxxvii No Author Stated, (No Date Stated), "The Importance of Pilot Projects in AI Implementation" published at wizata.com.

clxxxviii Turner, D., (2025), "The 30% Club: Why Most Digital Transformations Fail - And How AI Can Help," published by *LinkedIn Articles* at linkedIn.com.

clxxxix Ameisen, E., (2020), *Building Machine Learning Powered Applications: Going from Idea to Product*, O'Reilly Media.

cxc Domingos, P., (2015), *The Master Algorithm: How the Quest for the Ultimate Learning Machine Will Remake Our World,* Basic Books.

cxci Christensen, C. M., (2011), *"The Innovator's Dilemma: When New Technologies Cause Great Firms to Fail,"* Harper Business.

cxcii Davenport, T. H., & Harris, J. H., (2017), *Competing on Analytics: The New Science of Winning*, Harvard Business Review Press.

cxciii Pink, D. H., (2011), *Drive: The Surprising Truth About What Motivates Us*, Riverhead Books.

cxciv Provost, F., & Fawcett, T., (2013), *Data Science for Business: What You Need to Know about Data Mining and Data-Analytic Thinking*, O'Reilly Media; No Author Stated, (No Date Stated), "What are Data Silos?" published at talend.com.

cxcv O'Neil, C., *Weapons of Math Destruction: How Big Data Increases Inequality and Threatens Democracy*. Crown, 2016.

cxcvi Mayer-Schönberger, V., & Cukier, K., (2013), *Big Data: A Revolution That Will Transform How We Live, Work, and Think*, Harper Business.

cxcvii Kotter, J. P., (2012), *Leading Change*, Harvard Business Review Press.

cxcviii Finio, M., & Downie, A., (2024), "How to Scale AI in Your Organization" published at ibm.com.

cxcix U.S. AI Safety Institute Technical Staff, (2025), "Technical Blog: Strengthening AI Agent Hijacking Evaluations" published at nist.gov.

cc Schneier, B., (2016), *Data and Goliath: The Hidden Battles to Collect Your Data and Control Your World*, W.W. Norton & Company.

cci Lee, N., Resnick, P., & Barton, G., (2019), "Algorithmic bias detection and mitigation: Best practices and policies to reduce consumer harms" published at brookings.edu; Hobson, S., & Dortch, A., (2021), "Mitigating Bias in Artificial Intelligence" published at ibm.com.

[ccii] O'Neil, C., (2016), *Weapons of Math Destruction: How Big Data Increases Equality and Threatens Democracy*, Crown; McKenna, M., (No Date Stated), "Machines and Trust: How to Mitigate AI Bias" published at toptal.com.

[cciii] Miller, K., (2024), "Privacy in an AI Era: How Do We Protect Our Personal Information?" published at hai.stanford.edu; Gomstyn, A., & Jonker, A., (2024), "Exploring privacy issues in the age of AI" published at ibm.com; Valenzuela, A., (2024), "What is Data Anonymization? Techniques, Tools, and Best Practices Explained" published at datacamp.com.

[cciv] Rodrigues, R., & Papakonstantinou, (2018), *Privacy and Data Protection Seals*, T.M.C. Asser Press; No Author Stated, (2024), "What Are Privacy-Enhancing Technologies (PETs) and How Do They Work?" published at em360tech.com; No Author Stated, (2024), "Exploring Practical Considerations and Applications for Privacy Enhancing Technologies" published at isaca.org; Subramanian, R., (2023), "Have the cake and eat it too: Differential Privacy enables privacy and precise analytics" published by the *Journal of Big Data*, 10(117), and at journalofbigdata.springeropen.com; Kaur, H., Rani, V., Kumar, M., Sachdeva, M., Mittal, A., & Kumar, K., (2024), "Federated learning: a comprehensive review of recent advances and applications" published by *Multimedia Tools and Applications*, 83, and at link.spring.com.

[ccv] Rodrigues, R., & Papakonstantinou, (2018), *Privacy and Data Protection Seals*, T.M.C. Asser Press; No Author Stated, (2024), "What Are Privacy-Enhancing Technologies (PETs) and How Do They Work?" published at em360tech.com.

[ccvi] Kime, C. & Lafferty, M. (contributor), (2024), "Strong Encryption Explained: 6 Encryption Best Practices" published at esecurityplanet.com.

[ccvii] Javaid, U., (2024), "Data Anonymization: Definition, Types, Applications, Pros, and Cons" published at betterdata.ai; Wickramasinghe, S., (2021), "What's Data Masking? Types, Techniques & Best Practices" published at bmc.com; No Author Stated, (2023 but Updated in 2024), "What is tokenization?" published at mckinsey.com.

[ccviii] Ben-Ari, D., (2023), "Why Do Organizations Need Granular Permission Control?" published at panorays.com; McCarthy, M., (No Date Stated but Updated in 2025), "The Definitive Guide to Role-Based Access Control (RBAC)" published at strongdm.com; Siddiqui, M., (2024), "Attribute-Based Access Control (ABAC) - A Modern Approach to Dynamic and Granular Security" published at mdmteam.org.

[ccix] Khan, T., Tanjaya, A., Pratt, J., & Howell, J., (2024), "Transparency Through Documentation: A Pathway to Safer AI" published at partnershiponai.org; Jonker, A., Gomstyn, A., & Mcgrath, A., (2024), "What is AI transparency?" published at ibm.com; Brasse, J., Broder, H., Förster, Klier, M., & Sigler, I.,

(2023), "Explainable artificial intelligence in information systems: A review of the status quo and future research directions," *Electron Markets,* published at link.springer.com; Shin, T., (2024), "Understanding Feature Importance in Machine Learning" published at builtin.com; No Author Stated, (2025), "Decision Trees in Machine Learning: Two Types (+ Examples)" published at coursera.com.

[ccx] Khan, T., Tanjaya, A., Pratt, J., & Howell, J., (2024), "Transparency Through Documentation: A Pathway to Safer AI" published at partnershiponai.org; Jonker, A., Gomstyn, A., & Mcgrath, A., (2024), "What is AI transparency?" published at ibm.com; Marinos, T., & Gela, M., (No Date Stated), "Responsible AI: The Role of Data and Model Cards" published at datatonic.com; No Author Stated, (No Date Stated), "The Dataset Nutrition Label" published at datanutrition.org.

[ccxi] Molnar, C., (2022), *Interpretable Machine Learning: A Guide for Making Black Box Models Explainable*, Independently Published; Pappu, N., (No Date Stated), "AI Explainability 101; Making AI Decisions Transparent and Understandable" published at zendata.dev; Tada, (2024), "LIME (Local Interpretable Model-agnostic Explanations)" published at aicritique.org; Awan, A., (2023), "An Introduction to SHAP Values and Machine Learning Interpretability" published at datacamp.com; Sheikh, M., (2024), "Interactive Data Visualization: Examples, Techniques & Tools" published at vsme.co.

[ccxii] Jonker, A., Gomstyn, A., & McGrath, A., (2024), "What is AI transparency?" published at ibm.com; Blackman, R., & Ammanath, B., (2022), "Building Transparency into AI Projects" published by *Harvard Business Review* at hbr.org.

[ccxiii] Novelli, C., Taddeo, M., & Floridi, L., (2024), "Accountability in artificial intelligence: what it is and how it works," published at *AI & Society*, 39, and at link.springer.com; No Author Stated, (2024), "AI Accountability Policy Report" published at ntia.gov.

[ccxiv] Kearns, M. & Roth, A., (2019), *the ethical algorithm,* Oxford University Press; No Author Stated, (2022), "Microsoft Responsible AI Standard, v2" published at blogs.microsoft.com.

[ccxv] Novelli, C., Taddeo, M., & Floridi, L., (2024), "Accountability in artificial intelligence: what it is and how it works" published by *AI & Society*, 39, and at link.springer.com.

[ccxvi] Novelli, C., Taddeo, M., & Floridi, L., (2024), "Accountability in artificial intelligence: what it is and how it works," published at *AI & Society*, 39, and at link.springer.com; No Author Stated, (2024), "AI Accountability Policy Report" published at ntia.gov; Smith, G., Stanley, K., Marcinek, K., Cormarie, P., & Gunashekar, S., (2024), "Liability for Harms from AI Systems: The Application

of U.S. Tort Law and Liability to Harms from Artificial Intelligence Systems"
published at rand.org; Kelly, P., Walsh, M., Wyzykiewicz, S., & Young-Alls, S.,
(2021), "Man vs. Machine: Legal liability in Artificial Intelligence contracts and
the challenges that can arise" published at dlapiper.com; Hacker, P., Krestel, R.,
Grundmann, S., & Naumann, F., (2020), "Explainable AI under contract and tort
law: legal incentives and technical challenges" published by *Artificial
Intelligence and Law*, 28, and at link.springer.com.

ccxvii Novelli, C., Taddeo, M., & Floridi, L., (2024), "Accountability in artificial
intelligence: what it is and how it works," published at *AI & Society*, 39, and at
link.springer.com; Lakewoods, C., (2025), "Building Secure and Ethical AI
Systems for Innovation" published at techbullion.com.

ccxviii No Author Stated, (2023); "Necessity of Informed Consent for Data-Centric
AI" published at futurebeeai.com; Cascella, L., (No Date Stated), "Artificial
Intelligence and Informed Consent" published at medpro.com.

ccxix Novelli, C., Taddeo, M., & Floridi, L., (2024), "Accountability in artificial
intelligence: what it is and how it works," published at *AI & Society*, 39, and at
link.springer.com; Lakewoods, C., (2025), "Building Secure and Ethical AI
Systems for Innovation" published at techbullion.com.

ccxx Liao, S.M., (2020), *Ethics of Artificial Intelligence*, Oxford University Press;
No Author Stated, (2023); "Ethical impact assessment: a tool of the
Recommendation on the Ethics of Artificial Intelligence" published at
unesdoc.unesco.org.

ccxxi Chui, M., Harrysson, M., Manyika, J., Roberts, R., Chung, R., Nel, P., & Van
Heteren, A., (2018), "Applying artificial intelligence for social good" published
by mckinsey.com; Sandle, T., (2025), "How to build AI as a force for social
good" published at digitaljournal.com.

ccxxii Shneiderman, B., (2022), *Human-Centered AI*, Oxford University Press; No
Author Stated, (2024), "Building Human-Centric AI Applications: A Step-by-
Step Guide" published by opendatascience.com.

ccxxiii Bostrom, N., & Yudkowsky, E., (2014), *The ethics of artificial intelligence*,
Cambridge University Press; Coeckelbergh, M., (2020), *AI Ethics,* The MIT
Press; No Author Stated, (No Date Stated), "AI Audits: Ensuring Ethical &
Effective AI" published at singlestoneconsulting.com.

ccxxiv Floridi, L, (2023), *The Ethics of Artificial Intelligence,* Oxford University
Press; No Author Stated, (2024), "AI regulations around the world: Trends,
takeaways & what to watch heading into 2025" published at diligent.com; No
Author Stated, (2025), "A global AI cheat sheet: comparing AI regulations
across key regions" published at gcore.com.

ccxxv Solove, D., & Schwartz, P., (2023), *Information Privacy Law,* Aspen
Publishing; No Author Stated, (No Date Stated but Updated in 2023), "Guidance

on AI and data protection" published by ico.org.uk; No Author Stated, (No Date Stated), "GDPR Compliance in the Age of Artificial Intelligence: Challenge and Solutions" published at gdpr-advisor.com.

[ccxxvi] No Author Stated, (No Date Stated but Updated in 2024), "California Consumer Privacy Act (CCPA)" published at oag.ca.gov.

[ccxxvii] Wolford, B., (No Date Stated), "A guide to GDPR data privacy requirements" published at gdpr.eu.

[ccxxviii] No Author Stated, No Date Stated, "PDPA Overview" published at pdpc.gov.sg.

[ccxxix] No Author Stated, No Date Stated, "The Personal Information Protection and Electronic Documents Act (PIPEDA)" published at priv.gc.ca.

[ccxxx] No Author Stated (2018 but Updated 2020), "Brazilian General Data Protection Law (LGPD, English Translation)" published at iapp.org.

[ccxxxi] No Author Stated, No Date Stated, "Data protection" published at gov.uk.

[ccxxxii] No Author Stated, No Date Stated, "Health Insurance Portability and Accountability Act of 1996 (HIPAA)" published at cdc.gov.

[ccxxxiii] Bharati, R., (2024), "AI and intellectual property: Legal frameworks and future directions" published in *International Journal of Law, Justice and Jurisprudence*, 4(2), and at lawjournal.info; Caldwell, K., (2025), "IP Protection in the Age of AI: What's Coming?" published at caldwelllaw.com and law.com.

[ccxxxiv] No Author Stated, (2024), "Copyright Ownership of Generative AI Output Varies Around the World" published at cooley.com.

[ccxxxv] Appel, G., Neelbauer, J., & Schweidel, D., (2023), "Generative AI Has an Intellectual Problem" published by *Harvard Business Review* at hbr.org.

[ccxxxvi] No Author Stated, (2024), "Copyright Ownership of Generative AI Output Varies Around the World" published at cooley.com.

[ccxxxvii] Golbin, I., (2021), "Algorithmic impact assessments: What are they and do you need them?" published at pwc.com.

[ccxxxviii] Farmer, J., & DeMicco, T., (2024), "Ensuring AI Accountability Through Product Liability: The EU Approach and Why American Businesses Should Care" published by *The National Law Review* at natlawreview.com.

[ccxxxix] Farmer, J., & DeMicco, T., (2024), "Ensuring AI Accountability Through Product Liability: The EU Approach and Why American Businesses Should Care" published by *The National Law Review* at natlawreview.com.

[ccxl] No Author Stated, (2024), "Liability Issues in AI: Who is Responsible When AI Fails?" published by generisonline.com.

[ccxli] No Author Stated, (2024), "Liability Issues in AI: Who is Responsible When AI Fails?" published by generisonline.com.

[ccxlii] Golbin, I., (2021), "Algorithmic impact assessments: What are they and do you need them?" published at pwc.com.

[ccxliii] Cwik, C.,, Suarez, C., & Thomson, L., (2024), *Artificial Intelligence: Legal Issues, Policy, and Practical Strategies,* American Bar Association;

[ccxliv] Dabah, G., (2023), "What is Data Minimization? Main Principles & Techniques" published at piiano.com.

[ccxlv] Kostic, N., (2024), "15 Secure Data Storage Solutions to Protect Your Data" published at phoenixnap.com.

[ccxlvi] No Author Stated, (2024), "Data Classification: Standards and Best Practices Guide" published at shinydocs.com.

[ccxlvii] Lee, P., (2025), "Synthetic Data and the Future of AI" published by the *Cornell Law Review* at publications.lawschool.cornell.edu.

[ccxlviii] Bailey, C., Mazz, R., Hass, D., & Buckgit, A., (2024), "Get started with data lifecycle management" published at learn.microsoft.com.

[ccxlix] Sargiotis, D., (2024), "Data Stewardship and Ownership: Best Practices" chapter in the book *Data Governance* published by Springer and at link.springer.com.

[ccl] No Author Stated, (2024), "Data Security 101: Training Employees to Keep Company Data Safe" published at trinet.com.

[ccli] No Author Stated, (No Date Stated), "Creating a Data Breach Response Plan - Complete Guide" published at sealpath.com.

[cclii] Jessen, J., (2025), "WEF: AI will Create and Displace Millions of Jobs" published at sustainabilitymag.com; Kelly, J., (2023), "Goldman Sachs Predicts 300 Million Jobs Bill Be Lost Or Degraded By Artificial Intelligence" published at forbes.com.

[ccliii] Frey, C. B., & Osborne, M., (2013), "The Future of Employment: How Susceptible Are Jobs to Computerization?" Published at Oxford University Press at oxfordmartin.ox.ac.uk.

[ccliv] Brynjolfsson, E., & McAfee, A., (2016), *The Second Machine Age: Work, Progress, and Prosperity in a Time of Brilliant Technologies*, W. W. Norton & Company.

[cclv] Davenport, T. H., & Kirby, J., (2016), *Only Humans Need Apply: Winners and Losers in the Age of Smart Machines*, Harper Business.

[cclvi] Chui, M., Manyika, J., & Miremadi, M., (2016), "Where Machines Could Replace Humans—and Where They Can't (Yet)" published at mckinsey.com.

[cclvii] No Author Stated, (2025), "Transforming Manufacturing with AI: Optimizing Operations & Quality" published at tekrowe.com.

[cclviii] Topol, E., (2019), *Deep Medicine: How Artificial Intelligence Can Make Healthcare Human Again*, Basic Books.

[cclix] Spencer, A., (2024), "Artificial Intelligence in Retail: 6 Use Cases and Examples" published at forbes.com.

[cclx] Sidoti, G., (2024), "The Transformative Impact Of AI On Financial Services" published at forbes.com.

[cclxi] Brown, S., (2021), "Machine learning, explained" published at mitsloan.mit.edu.

[cclxii] Han, J., Kamber, Pei, J., & Tong, H., (2022), *Data Mining: Concepts and Techniques (4th Edition)*, Morgan Kaufmann.

[cclxiii] Coursera Staff, (No Date Stated but Updated in 2025), "AI in Software Development: Revolutionizing the Coding Landscape" published at coursera.org.

[cclxiv] Fisher, A., (2011), *Critical Thinking: An Introduction (2nd Edition)*, Cambridge University Press.

[cclxv] Goldsmith, M., (2016), *Triggers: Creating Behavior That Lasts--Becoming the Person You Want to Be*, Crown Business.

[cclxvi] Goleman, D., (2005), *Emotional Intelligence: Why It Can Matter More Than IQ*, Bantam Books.

[cclxvii] Westerman, G., Bonnet, D., & McAfee, A., (2014), *Leading Digital: Turning Technology into Business Transformation*, Harvard Business Review Press.

[cclxviii] Yermak, V., (2024), "Digital Tools and Technologies for Business Development" published at technorely.com.

[cclxix] Bostrom, N., & Yudkowsky, E., (2011), "The Ethics of Artificial Intelligence" published at nickbostrom.com.

[cclxx] Nayak, V., (2024), "How AI Is Revolutionizing Employee Training: Efficiency, Personalization, And Engagement" published at elearningindustry.com.

[cclxxi] Curry, R., (2023), "On-the-job generative AI training is already critical for workers. Here's how to get started" published at cnbc.com.

[cclxxii] Badawi, S., (2024), "How to Build Collaborative Educational Partnerships Across Institutions" published at adam.ai.

[cclxxiii] Porter, R., (2025), "How AI Is Shaping the Future of Corporate Training in 2025" published at trainingindustry.com.

[cclxxiv] Capone, M., (2025), "Why Leaders Should Let Employees Experiment More With AI" published at forbes.com.

[cclxxv] Brynjolfsson, E., & McAfee, A., (2016), *The Second Machine Age: Work, Progress, and Prosperity in a Time of Brilliant Technologies*, W. W. Norton & Company; Chamorro-Premuzic, T., (2020), "Why You Should Become an Intrapreneur" published by the *Harvard Business Review* at hbr.org.

[cclxxvi] Bostrom, N., & Yudkowsky, E., (2011), "The Ethics of Artificial Intelligence" published at nickbostrom.com.

[cclxxvii] Tripathi, A. & Kumar, V., (2025), "Ethical practices of artificial intelligence: a management framework for responsible AI deployment in businesses" published by *AI and Ethics* and at link.springer.com.

[cclxxviii] Marr, B., (2024), "How to Measure AI Success in Your Organization" published at forbes.com.

[cclxxix] Marr, B., (2024), "How to Measure AI Success in Your Organization" published at forbes.com.

[cclxxx] Shukla, M. (2024), "The Evolution Of Process Automation In The AI Era" published at forbes.com.

[cclxxxi] Langley, K., (No Date Stated), "How can I measure the impact of AI automation on my productivity?" published at kentlangley.com.

[cclxxxii] Barr, S., (No Date Stated), "Measuring the Cost and Return on Investment (ROI) with AI Implementation" published at bhmpc.com.

[cclxxxiii] Ataman, A., (2025), "Data Quality in AI: Challenges, Importance & Best Practices ['25]" published at research.aimultiple.com.

[cclxxxiv] Kerchner, A., (No Date Stated), "Key AI and Automation Success Metrics for Measuring Effectiveness" published at inkyma.com.

[cclxxxv] Koduvalli, M., (2024), "The ultimate guide to enterprise AI model evaluation" published at invisible.co.

[cclxxxvi] Davison, E., (No Date Stated), "Chapter 9: Measuring Success - Key Performance Indicators (KPIs) for AI Initiatives" published at tellmeprompter.com.

[cclxxxvii] No Author Stated, (No Date Stated), "AI Powered Visual Inspection" published at sorsys.ca.

[cclxxxviii] Ucar, A., Karakose, M., & Kırımça, N., (2024), "Artificial Intelligence for Predictive Maintenance Applications: Key Components, Trustworthiness, and Future Trends" published by *Applied Sciences*, 14(2), and at mdpi.com.

[cclxxxix] Maoz, M., (2025), "AI in Customer Experience: How to Stay Ahead" published by salesforce.com.

[ccxc] Saadioui, Z., (2024), "How to Measure Customer Satisfaction in AI Interactions" published at arsturn.com.

[ccxci] Thomas, M., (No Date Stated), "How to Use Generative AI to Encourage High NPS and Customer Loyalty" published at forethought.ai.

ccxcii No Author Stated, (2023), *Flip the AI Switch to Brilliant Customer Satisfaction* published by NICE Systems at get.nice.com.

ccxciii No Author Stated, (2023), *Flip the AI Switch to Brilliant Customer Satisfaction* published by NICE Systems at get.nice.com.

ccxciv Olivia, (2024), "Measuring the ROI of AI in Customer Support: Tangible Results and Timelines" published at entrepreneurshiplife.com.

ccxcv Chinoy, H. & Liu, A., (2024), "Measuring gen AI success: A deep dive into the KPIs you need" published at cloud.google.com.

ccxcvi Chinoy, H., & Liu, A., (2024), "Measuring gen AI success: A deep dive into the KPIs you need to know" published at cloud.google.com.

ccxcvii Pawar, S., (2023), "How To Transform Data Into Actionable Insights With Machine Learning" published at analyticsdrift.com.

ccxcviii No Author Stated, (2024), "AI Powered Dashboards: Transform Insights into Action with Maximize Impact" published at quantizig.com; Desai, M., (2024), "Optimizing Performance with Artificial Intelligence Dashboards" published at ezinsights.ai.

ccxcix York, A., (2025), "Make Informed Decisions: 10 First-Class AI Tools for Data Visualization" published at clickup.com.

ccc No Author Stated, (2023), "13 Components for Successful Performance Measurement" published at synergita.com.

ccci Sokolova, M., & Lapalme, G., (2009), "A systematic analysis of performance measures for classification tasks" published in *Information Processing & Management* and at researchgate.net.

cccii Powers, D., (2020), "Evaluation: from precision, recall and F-measure to ROC, informedness, markedness and correlation" arXiv:2010.16061 published at arxiv.org; No Author Stated, (No Date Stated), "Understanding the F1 Score: Definition, Importance, Calculation" published at futuremachinelearning.org.

ccciii Kundu, R., (2022), "Confusion Matrix: How to Use It & Interpret Results [Examples]" published at v7labs.com.

ccciv s-polly, & sdgilley, (2024), "A/B Experiments for AI applications" published at learn.microsoft.com.

cccv No Author Stated, (No Date Stated), "A/B Testing" published at optimizely.com.

cccvi Andreazzi, F., (2024), "Conversion Rate: What It Is, How to Calculate It, and What Is the Ideal Conversion Rate?" published at getleadster.com.

cccvii No Author Stated, (2024), "The Power of AI Feedback Loop: Learning From Mistakes" published at irisagent.com.

cccviii Barry, P., (2023), *Feedback Loops: Feedback Fundamentals*, published by Michigan Publishing Services.

[cccix] Bergmann, D., & Stryker, C., (2025), "What is model training?" published at ibm.com.

[cccx] Hermans, K., (2023), *Mastering AI Model Training: A Comprehensive Guide to Become an Expert in Training AI Models*, independently published.

[cccxi] Bayoumi, A., (2024), "A Comprehensive Guide to Incremental Learning in AI" published at aiixx.ai.

[cccxii] No Author Stated, (No Date Stated but Updated in 2025), "Incremental Development Model in Agile AI" published at restack.io.

[cccxiii] Reuel, A., Hardy, A., Smith, C., Lamparth, M., Hardy, M., & Kochenderfer, M., (2024), "BetterBench: A repository of AI benchmark assessments for informed benchmark selection through quality evaluation and best practice analysis" published at betterbench.standford.edu; Reuel, A., Hardy, A., Smith, C., Lamparath, M., Hardy, M., & Kochenderfer, M., (2024), "What Makes a Good AI Benchmark?" published at hai.stansford.edu.

[cccxiv] Bergmann, D., (2024), "The most important AI trends in 2024" published at ibm.com; No Author Stated, (No Date Stated), "Future of AI: How 10 Emerging Trends are Transforming Industries" published at startus-insights.com.

[cccxv] How, M., & Cheah, S., (2024), "Forging the Future: Strategic Approaches to Quantum AI Integration for Industry Transformation" published at mdpi.com.

[cccxvi] Hemmati, A., Raoufi, P., & Rahmani, A., (2024), "Edge artificial intelligence for big data: a systematic review" published in *Neural Computing and Applications* and at link.springer.com.

[cccxvii] No Author Stated, (No Date Stated), "Exploring Edge AI: Implementing Artificial Intelligence Directly on Edge Devices" published at algocademy.com.

[cccxviii] Brasse, J., Broder, H., Förster, Klier, M., & Sigler, I., (2023), "Explainable artificial intelligence in information systems: A review of the status quo and future research directions," *Electron Markets,* published at link.springer.com.

[cccxix] No Author Cited, (No Date Stated), "The Impact of AI on Biotechnology: Revolutionizing the Future of Medicine" published at sequencebiotech.com; No Author Cited, (No Date Cited), "AI in Biotechnology: 10 Practical Use Cases You Need to Know (2025 & Beyond)" published at startus-insights.com.

[cccxx] Qureshi, B., (2023), "AI - The Future of Biotechnology and Healthcare" published at scientiamag.org.

[cccxxi] Spleiss, C., (2025), "AI in Agriculture: Smarter Crops, Healthier Livestock, Better Yields" published at cloudsecurityalliance.org.

[cccxxii] Shuliak, M., (2025), "Artificial Intelligence and Renewable Energy: A Guide to Tech Sustainability" published at acropolium.com.

[cccxxiii] Murari, H., (2024), "AI for Climate Change: Innovative Models Predicting Environmental Impact" in *Smart Data News, Articles, & Education* and published at dataversity.net.

[cccxxiv] Atwater, C., (2023), "The Future of Creativity: How Generative AI is Transforming Art, Music and Design" published at robots.net.

[cccxxv] Team EMB, (2024), "The Role of AI in Music Composition and Production" published at blog.emb.global/ai-in-music-composition-and-production/.

[cccxxvi] Bolaños,. F., Salatino, A., Osborne, F., & Motta, E., (2024), "Artificial Intelligence for literature reviews: opportunities and challenges" published in the *Artificial Intelligence Review* 57(529) and at link.springer.com.

[cccxxvii] De Hoog, G., (2025), "Sensory augmentation" published at elitacwearables.com.

[cccxxviii] No Author Stated, (2025), "The Role of AI in Workplace Technology: 10 Ways Companies Are Maximizing its Impact" published at cbre.com.

[cccxxix] Girimonte, M., (2024), "How AI is Redefining Interactive Storytelling" published at voices.com.

[cccxxx] RoX818, (2025), "Emotionally Intelligent AI Agents: Empathy Meets Innovation" published at aicompetence.org.

[cccxxxi] Hadiyana, T., & Ji-hoon, S., (2024), "AI-Driven Urban Planning: Enhancing Efficiency and Sustainability in Smart Cities" published in *Information Technology Engineering Journals* and at syeknurjati.ac.id.

[cccxxxii] Klein, A., (2024), "Mind-Machine Interfaces (MMIs)" published at charlesaustinklein.com.

[cccxxxiii] Nagar, A., Morrison, P., & Chalapathy, P., (2024), "How AI Fuels Hyperpersonalization in Retail Experiences" published at wns.com.

[cccxxxiv] Eapen, T., Finkenstadt, D., Folk, J., & Venkataswamy, L., (2023), "How Generative AI Can Augment Human Creativity" published by *Harvard Business Review* at hbr.org.

[cccxxxv] Hoskins, A., (2024), "AI and memory" published by Cambridge University at cambridge.com.

[cccxxxvi] Tuzhilin, A., (2024), "Navigating the Ethical Challenges of AI: A Guide for Tech Leaders" published at uopeople.edu.

[cccxxxvii] Mucci, T., & Stryker, C., (2024), "What is AI governance?" published at ibm.com.

[cccxxxviii] Manyika, J., Silberg, J., & Presten, B., (2019), "What Do We Do About the Biases in AI?" published by *Harvard Business Review* at hbr.org.

[cccxxxix] Seung, Y., & Basham, J., (No Date Stated), "Conceptualizing AI Literacy: A Critical Skill for the 21st Century" published at ciddl.org.

[cccxl] Kent, J., (2025), "How to Keep Up with AI Through Reskilling" published at professional.dce.harvard.edu; Chen, C., (2025), "Level Up: Training Employees to Work Alongside AI" published at traningindustry.com.

cccxli Bisconti, P., Orsitto, D., Fedorczyk, F., Brau, F., Capasso, M., De Marinis, L., Eken, H., Merenda, F., Forti, M., Pacini, M., & Schettini, C., (2023), "Maximizing team synergy in AI-related interdisciplinary groups: an interdisciplinary-by-design iterative methodology" published by *AI & Society*, 38, and at link.springer.com.

cccxlii Sharma, R., (2024), "How public-private partnerships can ensure ethical, sustainable and inclusive AI development" published at weforum.org.

cccxliii Sharma, R., (2024), "How public-private partnerships can ensure ethical, sustainable and inclusive AI development" published at weforum.org.

cccxliv Flinders, M., & Smalley, I., (2024), "What is AI Infrastructure?" published at ibm.com; No Author Stated, (2024), "AI infrastructure: a comprehensive guide to building your AI stack" published at future-processing.

cccxlv RoX818, (2024), "Emerging AI Hubs: Countries Poised to Shape the Future of AI" published at aicompetence.org; Chakravorti, B., Bhalla, A., Chaturvedi, R., Filipovic, C., (2021), "50 Global Hubs for Top AI Talent" published by *Harvard Business Review* at hbr.org.

cccxlvi No Author Stated, (2023), "Regulatory sandboxes in artificial intelligence" published at oecd.org.

cccxlvii Sukhadeve, A., (2021), "Artificial Intelligence For Good: How AI Is Helping Humanity" published at forbes.com.

cccxlviii Bisconti, P., Orsitto, D., Fedorczyk, Brau, F., Capasso, M., De Marinis, L., Eken, H., Merenda, F., Forti, M., Pacini, M., & Schettini, C., (2023), "Maximizing team synergy in AI-related interdisciplinary groups: an interdisciplinary-by-design iterative methodology" published by *AI & Society*, 38, and at link.springer.com.

cccxlix No Author Stated, (No Date Stated), "The Importance of Continuous Learning in AI: Navigating Technological Evolution" published at profiletree.com.

cccl No Author Stated, (No Date Stated but Updated in 2025), "Processing? Definition, Types, and Examples" published at spiceworks.com.

www.ingramcontent.com/pod-product-compliance
Lightning Source LLC
LaVergne TN
LVHW051434050326
832903LV00030BD/3084